ELIZABETH BOWEN

Women Writers

General Editors: *Eva Figes and Adele King*

Published titles:

Sylvia Plath, Susan Bassnett
Fanny Burney, Judy Simons
Christina Stead, Diana Brydon
Charlotte Brontë, Pauline Nestor
Margaret Atwood, Barbara Hill Rigney
Eudora Welty, Louise Wrestling
Anne Brontë, Elizabeth Langland
Women in Romanticism, Meena Alexander
Willa Cather, Susie Thomas
Elizabeth Bowen, Phyllis Lassner
Emily Brontë, Lyn Pykett

Forthcoming:

Jane Austen, Meenakshi Mukherjee
Elizabeth Barrett Browning, Marjorie Stone
Ivy Compton Burnett, Kathy Gentile
Colette, Diana Holmes
Emily Dickinson, Joan Kirkby
George Eliot, Kristin Brady
Mrs Gaskell, Jane Spencer
Doris Lessing, Barbara Hill Rigney
Katherine Mansfield, Diana DeBell
Christina Rossetti, Linda Marshall
Jean Rhys, Carol Rumens
Muriel Spark, Judith Sproxton
Edith Wharton, Katherine Joslin
Virginia Woolf, Clare Hanson

Women Writers

ELIZABETH BOWEN

Phyllis Lassner

MACMILLAN

First published 1990

Published by
MACMILLAN EDUCATION LTD
Houndmills, Basingstoke, Hampshire RG21 2XS
and London
Companies and representatives
throughout the world

Printed in Hong Kong

British Library Cataloguing in Publication Data
Lassner, Phyllis
  Elizabeth Bowen– (Women writers)
  I. Title II. Series
  823'.912

  ISBN 0–333–44253–9
  ISBN 0–333–44254–7 Pbk

Contents

Acknowledgements

Writing this book became as much a pleasure as a challenge because of the help I received from two people. Mickey Pearlman read each chapter and responded with all the tough and astute criticism I have come to expect from my favourite editor. Jacob Lassner gave me a year off in exotic and wonderful places to write this book and many other years of infinite support and encouragement.

The author and publishers wish to thank the following for permission to use copyright material:

Jonathan Cape Ltd. on behalf of the Estate of Elizabeth Bowen for extracts from *The Last September*, *To the North*, *Friends and Relations*, *The Heat of the Day*, *The House in Paris* and *The Death of the Heart* by Elizabeth Bowen.

Curtis Brown Ltd. on behalf of the Estate of Elizabeth Bowen for extracts from 'The Forgotten Art of Living' by Elizabeth Bowen from *Good Living* ed. A.G. Eidenfeld. Copyright © 1948 by Elizabeth Bowen; *Seven Winters* by Elizabeth Bowen. Copyright ©1943 by Elizabeth Bowen; *Collected Impressions* by Elizabeth Bowen. Copyright © 1954 by Elizabeth Bowen; *Afterthought* by Elizabeth Bowen. Copyright ©1962 by Elizabeth Bowen; and unpublished writings, letter dated 2 August and two letters to Charles Ritchie.

Harcourt Brace Jovanovich for extracts from 'Why I Write', 'Coming to London' and 'The Bend Back' from *The Mulberry Tree* by Elizabeth Bowen. Copyright ©1986 by Curtis Brown Ltd., Literary Executors of the Estate of Elizabeth Bowen.

The Irish American Cultural Institute for extracts from 'The Past is a Burning Pattern: Elizabeth Bowen's *The Last September*', *Eire-Ireland*.

Alfred A. Knopf, Inc. for extracts from *The Last September*, *To the North*, *The House in Paris*, *The Death of the Heart*, *The Heat of the Day* and *Bowen's Court* by Elizabeth Bowen.

Virago Press Ltd. for extracts from 'Out of a Book', 'Origins', 'Places', 'The Mulberry Tree', 'Why I Write', 'Coming to London', 'Ivy Compton Burnett', 'She', 'Stories by Katherine Mansfield', 'Encounters', 'The Big House', 'Uncle Silas', 'The Bend Back', and 'Doubtful Subject', and Prefaces to 'Stories by Elizabeth Bowen', 'The Last September' and 'The Demon Lover', by Elizabeth Bowen from *The Mulberry Tree*, edited by Hermione Lee; for extracts from *Seven Winters* and *Bowen's Court* by Elizabeth Bowen.

For permission to quote from previously unpublished material, we are indebted to The Harry Ransom Humanities Research Center, The University of Texas at Austin for 'Women's Place in the Affairs of Men' and 'The Art of Reason or The Art of Respecting Boundaries'. The New York Public Library Henry W. and Alberta A. Berg Collection, Astor, Lenox and Tilden Foundations gave permission to quote from 'The Experience of Writing', notes to a lecture delivered at Wellesley College, 20 March 1950, Bowen's letter to May Sarton, 2 November 1937, and her letters to Virginia Woolf, 1 July 1940 and 26 August 1940.

Every effort has been made to trace all the copyright holders but if any have been inadvertently overlooked the publishers will be pleased to make the necessary arrangement at the first opportunity.

Editors' Preface

The study of women's writing has been long neglected by a male critical establishment both in academic circles and beyond. As a result, any women writers have either been unfairly neglected, or have been marginalised in some way, so that their true influence and importance has been ignored. Other women writers have been accepted by male critics and academics, but on terms which seem, to many women readers of this generation, to be false or simplistic. In the past the internal conflicts involved in being a woman in a male-dominated society have been largely ignored by readers of both sexes, and this has affected our reading of women's work. The time has come for a serious reassessment of women's writing in the light of what we understand today.

This series is designed to help in that reassessment.

All the books are written by women, because we believe that men's understanding of feminist critique is only, at best, partial. And besides, men have held the floor quite long enough.

EVA FIGES
ADELE KING

To Jake, Liz and Jason

1 Elizabeth Bowen's Life

> Complex people are never certain that they are not
> crooks, never certain their passports are quite in order[1]

Elizabeth Bowen's life story is as complex and intricately
balanced as her fiction. But if her female characters seem
uncertain in the face of traditional expectations, Bowen
fashioned her own creative energy into a powerful person-
ality which overcame personal and historic upheaval. It is
easy to picture her in London at the height of the Blitz,
juggling with great relish the roles of celebrity-artist, air-raid
warden, investigator for the Ministry of Information, lover,
wife, and writer of what are probably the best English stories
and novel of World War II. Elizabeth Bowen was 'a woman
of the world'. The vocabulary of her day describes her as
'sophisticated', a word always defined pejoratively by the
Oxford English Dictionary. But, like the strong female
characters celebrated in British and American films of
the 1940s, sophistication suggests a woman supremely
canny about the ways of the worlds in which she moved
and lived.

  Like these fictional women, Bowen was ambitious, intensely verbal and articulate, warm, self-contained and
self-knowing. She also possessed a strong sense of humour,
self-mocking as well as capable of mocking the pretensions
of others. If she sometimes appeared cynical, she was
fiercely devoted to friends, choosing and keeping them
because she knew exactly what they needed from each
other and how to accommodate the many layers of their
lives. Her gift for understanding and testing the constraints
of social and political codes merged with her imagination
to devise plots which overturned convention to highlight

1

a 'new woman's' energy. Elizabeth Bowen transformed an uneasy mix of two cultural identities, English and Irish, into a rich and fulfilling personal and professional life. Her adept and graceful manoeuvres between convention and a powerful sense of her own needs for expression would have daunted anyone less energetic. Until cancer destroyed her voice and strength and finally killed her in 1973, she was writing and enjoying the great love and friendships of her life.

A romantic, but never naive, Bowen understood the costs of inherited responsibilities and the desire to transform them into creative self-expression. In nearly fifty years of literary achievement, she envisioned this dilemma in fictions formed by an acute sense of history. In all of her work the pressures of social and family tradition shape the lives of characters who wish for or resist change. Her empathy for both adult and child characters reflects her deepest sense, as she records in her short story 'Coming Home', that 'There was no security. Safety and happiness were a game that grown-up people played with children to keep them from understanding'.[2]

Bowen's life and work show a keen pleasure as well as anxiety about the family and cultural heritage which haunts her consciousness as well as that of her characters. The ancestral home which she inherited represented a cultural and family history which in its extreme partisanships, expectations, rituals and losses, took on the shape of a myth. Bowen's biographers and critics rarely fail to point to the conservative, even reactionary strand in her work which they connect to her landed gentry background. Such a judgement fails to notice the deep but critical attachment Bowen felt towards her Anglo-Irish heritage. If she learned from her extravagant ancestors to live in great style, above all she felt the need to work. And it is in her work that she creates a jaundiced view of those who sacrifice the living for a sense of order formed by romanticised views of an inglorious past. That Bowen is a critic as novelist is endemic to her character. For although she was born to the manor, she knew it for what it was outside of myths:

No, it is not only our fate but our business to lose innocence, and once we have lost that it is futile to attempt a picnic in Eden.[3]

Elizabeth Bowen was not born in an Eden. By the time the only child of Florence Colley Bowen and Henry Cole Bowen was born in 1899, the ancestral home, Bowen's Court, had already suffered the ravages of family rancour and careless management and was now only a part-time residence. Bowen's father earned his living practising law in Dublin. The decision to have a profession instead of managing Bowen's Court was a rebellious move which earned his father's wrath and led to the final decline of the estate. Robert Cole Bowen left his son the house but without the lands which supported it. The tempestuous relations between Henry Bowen and his father Robert were the last in a history of family litigation and wilfulness that is easy to see as one more in a long line of Anglo-Irish Houses of Usher. The feelings of ghostliness, fatedness, ill deeds and vendettas are elements of a drama familiar to readers of Maria Edgeworth, Sheridan Le Fanu, even Poe, and contemporary sentimentalisers of gothic romance. It is clear the Bowen family felt themselves under the spell of such a myth, but it took the last heir, the only female heir to the big house, to both render the terms of such a myth and to demystify it:

What runs on most through a family living in one place is a continuous, semi-physical dream. Above this dream-level successive lives show their tips, their little conscious formations of will and thought. With the end of each generation, the lives that submerged here were absorbed again. With each death, the air of the place had thickened: it had been added to. The dead do not need to visit Bowen's Court rooms – as I said, we had no ghosts in that house – because they already permeated them. . . . The land outside Bowen's Court windows left prints on my ancestors' eyes that looked out: perhaps their eyes left, also, prints on the scene? If so, those prints were part of the scene for me.[4]

In her family chronicle, *Bowen's Court*, Bowen exorcises the ghosts which haunt her creative imagination by forming characters who feel dependent on family homes for their very lives. In so doing, she builds a psychological portrait of her family as entrenched in a self-made tradition they came to believe determined their lives. It is this combination of self-determination and fatedness that forms their character as they fight, plunder, build and decline, along with the rest of Anglo-Ireland.

The Bowen line is traced back to the Welsh apOwen who came to Ireland with the English conquests in the seventeenth century. It was not, however, until 1765, when a Bowen married into the wealthy Cole family, that Bowen's Court was built. Like many of their compatriots, the Bowens viewed their big house as a mark of their permanent status in Ireland. In political reality, it was a complex and conflicted sign of the Protestant Ascendancy, and the house came to symbolise separateness from Catholic Ireland and dual allegiance to Ireland and England. Political, religious and social exclusiveness was reinforced by the isolated location of the house in the south-eastern countryside of County Cork. Bowen later came to identify the isolation of the Anglo-Irish with her own life. They are 'only children who do not know how much they miss. Their existence, like those of only children, are singular, independent and secretive' (*BC* 20).

For Bowen, external isolation was exacerbated by a sense of personal isolation that was the consequence of being an only child to parents who seemed to live in a world of their own. She describes her mother as remote, a feature which is disturbing to the children of so many mothers in her fiction. Florence Bowen, according to her daughter's recollections, was frequently disengaged from the everyday events of the household and withdrawn in her own thoughts. This was only a continuation of Florence's behaviour in her own mother's home, where she had been considered something of a misfit, vague and yet temperamental in the cheerful, sociable world of the Colleys. In marrying Henry Bowen, Florence was able to be herself, completely compatible with a man who was 'unworldly, introspective, and scholarly'.[5]

Elizabeth Bowen was born nine years after her parents' marriage. Expecting a son, they had chosen the name Robert, but Elizabeth does not appear to have been a disappointment. Indeed, her presence seems to have captivated her mother, who saw to her daughter's social and academic lessons with great zeal. It was especially important to Florence that her child feel at home in all the social activities of Protestant Ireland that she herself had responded to more shyly. Dancing classes, parties and horse-riding lessons took priority along with a great concern not to tax a fragile disposition Florence assumed Elizabeth inherited from the Bowens. For this reason, although Elizabeth had a governess from early childhood, she was not taught to read until she was seven. Florence Bowen's intense devotion to her child was fraught with anxiety. A chief function of the governess was to discipline Elizabeth because Florence 'was so much desolated that she unnerved me when anything went wrong between her and me'.[6]

Absent-minded like his wife, Henry Bowen was also distracted by professional pressures. Already suffering his father's disapproval of his profession at the bar, Henry switched careers again. He became a searcher of complicated and heavily encumbered land titles, a painstaking and stressful job. At the same time he endured the pressures of keeping up his ancestral home which by now could no longer support itself. When her father was not working extremely long hours, Bowen's parents lived in a world of their own. Although each was loving to her, together, 'they each ruled their private kingdoms of thought, and inside it I . . . began to set up my own' (SW 11). Isolation, which therefore was endemic to Bowen's life, then took on an ominous cast.

When Bowen was seven years old her father suffered a mental breakdown. The symptoms were sufficiently severe, and very likely violent, that doctors and family recommended that Florence leave Ireland with her daughter to live near relatives at Hythe and Folkestone on the English coast. The move was traumatic for the child, separating her from her father and place of birth and robbing her forever of a sense of permanence and stability. The vague, remote mother who never noticed that anything was wrong with her husband was also unable to prepare her child for this crisis or any other. But Florence managed to pass on to her child a strategy for coping with crisis that found its way into the characters of Bowen's fiction. Mothers like Mrs Michaelis are both vigilant and inattentive, producing in their children, like Karen Michaelis, the capacity to act without anticipating consequences. At one time or another mothers and children in Bowen's fiction fail to notice what pains the other. They pass each other on the stairs, each withdrawn in her own fantasy, much like the Bowen couple who, as the story goes, once passed each other in their garden, never noticing the other's presence.

Such a strategy of passive withdrawal assumes political importance for Bowen's reconstruction of her family history and for her fiction. For just as the Anglo-Irish learned not to notice the peasants suffering and rebelling around their demesnes, so the Naylors in The Last September ignore the firing on their house until too late. They cling to the big house despite its liabilities, just as Henry Bowen struggled to keep Bowen's Court afloat. In Bowen's English novels, such defensive strategies focus on the politics of the family. Despite having left behind the revolutionary politics of Irish national life, Bowen shows that she felt deeply about the relations between the empowered and the powerless. She dramatises both the passion of those desiring power and the disenchantment of those discovering they are powerless. She not only seems to understand, indeed empathise, with both sides of this dilemma, she endows her dramatisations with extraordinary emotional depth and critique.

Although Florence Bowen seemed distracted and withdrawn when her daughter was very young, during the time they lived together in England, mother and daughter became intensely close and interdependent. The home they left behind was replaced by the intimate and loving relationship that grew between them. But the idyllic closeness ended tragically when Bowen was thirteen. Her mother developed cancer and died within a year. A cousin reported that Bowen 'never really got over it' (*VG* 32). The pain of separation from her father was now more than doubled by the loss of the mother who had formed her sense of nurture and emotional security. In fact, it could be said that although her father recovered and they became close after her mother's death, in her experience it was as though she had lost both parents. The presence of loss was apparent in the formation of a symptom that appeared with the disappearance of her father and was exacerbated at her mother's death. As she recalled much later, 'I had come out of the tension and mystery of my father's illness, the apprehensive silence or chaotic shoutings . . . with nothing more disastrous than a stammer'.[7] The stammer assumed a symbolic quality with her mother's death. As her cousin Audrey Fiennes reports, 'One of the words at which her stammer consistently baulked her was "mother" ' (*VG* 32). Related to the principle of 'not noticing', silence becomes both a coping strategy and the guarantor of anxiety, a way of not acknowledging pain and loss and yet reproducing it. When Florence Bowen died, her daughter was already afflicted with exile, parental loss, feelings of betrayal, and what she characterised in retrospect as 'total bereavement, a sense of disfigurement, mortification, disgrace'.[8]

The mysterious loss of parents, which is experienced as their silence, transmits an inability to find self-expression in the children of Bowen's fiction. In *The Death of the Heart* Portia Quayne's idyllic memories of cuddling with her mother under eiderdowns in seaside places recalls Bowen's time with her mother at Hythe and at Folkestone. But such memories are only partial truths, as they deny the hardships and insecurities of homelessness as well as the full story behind the decline and death of Portia's father. Portia's legacy is silence, the failure of anyone to tell her the real story of her birth and early life and to give her a sense of identity founded on actual events, not nostalgia.

For Bowen, the Edenic metaphor represents the place which is a memory of childhood unencumbered by realities of dispossession and loss and uncensored by critical glosses. The 'lies' which began as expressions of her parents' fears about their own frailties and which were perceived by Bowen as a symptom of their betrayal of her trust, were transformed into creative fictions. In this way she could safely recall childhood betrayal by penetrating the feelings which accompanied it. In her work she gained control over the domain she inherited. Writing overcame the silences which characterised her life while dramatising its crippling effects on fictive characters. The child of parents who were remote and preoccupied from the first, and then ill without explanation, had endured the most painful silence when her mother died. The stammer which resulted from these experiences did not, however, inhibit her powers of self-expression. She was not only known to be a clever and non-stop conversationalist, but she lectured both on the radio and in public. Most significantly, what could have been her own silence, was overcome by her art as a writer.

After her mother's death, Bowen was taken care of by a series of Colley aunts who also supervised her education. At Harpenden Hall her academic achievements were overshadowed by an adolescent delight at various fads, including one for the occult. Her summers at Bowen's Court were an occasion to indulge her energies even further, where 'towering periods of silliness' and 'vile scenes' were part of what Bowen felt were her 'instances of protracted childhood, which a furious selfishness reinforced'.[9] Glendinning sees childhood more resonant in Bowen's character than adolescence. Bowen's passionate enthusiasm for activity, her unvanquished disappointment when plans fell through, her directness and shyness were, she wrote, functions of 'the imaginative play thing a child has – that life isn't amusing enough, so you build it up with imagination of your own' (*VG* 36).

It was at Downe House, the girls' boarding-school in Kent which Bowen attended next, that she learned to trust her own originality and learned 'how not to write'.[10] Taken together, these qualities later ensured a style of sharply defined personal expression wedded to a sure knowledge of tradition and convention. As she wrote in *The Mulberry Tree*, her memoirs of these years, being sociable and 'farouche' meant that she could develop a style of her own that reflected 'a kind of inner irrational exaltation having little to do with morals one way or the other' (188).

Once she graduated from the Downe School, Bowen returned to Bowen's Court where her father was now living with his second wife, Mary Gwynne. Life at the big house now took on more of an actively social cast, with Bowen's high spirits complemented by the manners which were part of the curriculum at Downe House and by a quiet sense of order that Mary offered. Her life during these years

absorbed the social and political climate of Anglo-Ireland.
As she was to record later in her novel, *The Last September*,
the passion for sociability of the Anglo-Irish served to
camouflage the storm that was threatening the gates of
their demesnes. Like Lois, the twenty-year-old heroine
of that work, Bowen's only experience of the insurgency
surrounding her home was a short-lived romance with a
British soldier. If she was heartbroken over the broken
engagement, she understands such suffering in *The Last
September* in the dire context of a civilisation burning in its
own lassitude. Bowen's Court was spared, but the threat of
its destruction was a visceral experience for her. Although
she was travelling in Italy in 1921 when three houses in the
neighbourhood were burned, she responded by trying not
to imagine Bowen's Court in flames. The old strategy of
not noticing could only be useful as it was transformed into
The Last September. Sir Richard Naylor must stand impotent
while his big house burns at the novel's conclusion.

Like Lois Farquar, Bowen went off to London to
study art, but if we are not told what became of her
heroine, we know that for her creator, art was abandoned
in favour of writing. Unlike most Anglo-Irish debutantes,
Bowen could not tolerate a life spent primarily riding to the
hunt and preparing its accompanying social obligations. She
craved a professional life, seeing the writer as a 'Resistance
leader', who saw her art unpretentiously, as work that made
itself felt with the power of imaginative expression.[11] As in
her fiction, where she relentlessly demystified all romantic
impulses, she refused to see her emphasis on feeling as a
function of some kind of personal sensitivity. She was more
concerned with understanding the social and psychological
forces which produce intense feeling than with portraying
feeling as a lyrical exercise in purely expressionistic terms.
Although it is difficult to pin down a single, consistent
view of writing fiction from Bowen's often impression-
istic and seemingly contradictory statements, overall, it

becomes clear that for her, fantasy and intense emotion must be tempered by awareness of historical realities and their consequences in the manners and morals which characterise even fictive events. Her short stories are often 'visionary', representing concentrated sensation and fantasy, but 'the influence of the novel, with its calmer, stricter, more orthodox demands', provides the method for testing reality.[12]

Writing, for Bowen, has all the earmarks of a compulsion, but not one that reflects an impulse outside her control. Rather, it is a desire to give shape and clarity to feelings and experiences she would later describe as 'a phantasmagoric hinterland':

> Nothing made full sense to me that was not in print. Life seemed to promise to be intolerable without full sense, authoritative knowledge. Feeling what a book could do and what indeed only a book *could* do, made me wish to write: I conceived of nothing else as worth doing.[13]

Bowen wrote her first stories when she was twenty. They are a mixture of comedy of manners, the uncanny, and acutely portrayed emotional instants. They do not rely on any specific form for their subjects, but rather follow the tone of stories she most remembered reading. Certain themes emerge, however, which set the tone for the rest of her writing life. The child who suffers acute fear and anxiety at an absent and then absent-minded mother is given full play in 'Coming Home', while in 'Mrs Windermere', the relationship between older and younger women suggests the tensions that Bowen was to explore in many of her later works. Publication did not come instantly; editors of magazines rejected them one after the other. Only when Rose Macaulay, already successful as a novelist and critic, recognised their talent and introduced Bowen to the editor of the *Saturday Westminster*, did a growing network lead to acceptance by Rank Sidgwick. *Encounters* was published in 1923.

Bowen's professional success was followed almost immediately by marriage to Alan Cameron, an Assistant Secretary for Education. A talented administrator, Alan Cameron did not consider himself an intellectual and did not always fit into his wife's literary circles. He gets rather mixed reviews from her friends, remembered as a hearty Colonel Blimp. But this judgement reveals only the limited vision of the judges, not the character of the man. Among his professional colleagues, he was known to be 'exceptional and reassuring', qualities which made the marriage a success (*VG* 132–133). He was not only devoted to Elizabeth, but provided a ballast to her sometimes emotionally turbulent and professionally demanding life. The Camerons actually had great fun together. They loved to drive in the countryside for long stretches and shared a keen satiric sense of social pretension. He was the primary nurturer in her adult life, supporting her professional ambitions and creating a feeling of permanent emotional attachment on which they both could depend no matter what forces pulled her elsewhere. They had no children and in fact it could be said that they were parental to each other as they provided deep concern and love without sexual intensity.

In the first two years of their marriage Bowen wrote another collection of short stories, *Ann Lee's* and her first novel, *The Hotel*. For the first time since early childhood, she felt 'located', an experience of stability expressed as belonging to a place that so many of her fictional characters yearn for and never achieve (*VG* 61). *The Hotel* involves a group of people ostensibly on holiday, but actually transient in a more psychological sense. They are more attached to the small items which make travel comfortable than they are to people. Sydney Warren is the young heroine who becomes engaged impulsively only to break it off before she departs. She is in transit because she cannot find herself without the reassurance she needs in a relationship she strikes up with an older woman. The association of a mother-figure with the sense of a permanent place in which to grow prefigures Bowen's later fiction while recalling her experience of transience with her mother and the loss of her. Part of the importance of this novel to Bowen's development is her identification of a young woman's ambivalence about the direction of her life and the transformation of emotional intensity into comedy.

Making a family home was crucial to Bowen's creativity and in the home she made with Alan Cameron she was able to feel nourished and to work without interruption. Just as Bowen describes her parents' marriage as a 'place,' so her own became the holding environment which preceded in importance and informed every move the Camerons made. Thus it was with a sense of adventure and not disruption that they moved to Old Headington, near Oxford, when Alan became Secretary for Education for the city of Oxford. They lived in their stone converted coach-house, Waldencote, for ten years. It was here that Bowen formed the basis of personal and professional friendship that was to last a lifetime. The Camerons became close friends with John and Susan Buchan and it was at their home that Bowen met Virginia Woolf and Rosamond Lehmann. The proximity to the university gave Bowen access to other literary professionals, including David Cecil, then a don, who became well known for his literary criticism. Through Cecil she became friends with Maurice Bowra who in turn introduced her to Isaiah Berlin. These friendships were professional in the sense that they shared literary and cultural conversations, but they were also intensely devoted at a more emotional level. The Berlins were frequent visitors to Bowen's Court and after Alan Cameron's death, rented Bowen a flat they owned in Old Headington and provided great support and comfort.

Although Oxford has never been known for taking

up with creative artists, Bowen was a great hit. Her vitality and satiric sensibility, her no-nonsense attitude about individual morality and abstract principles made her a favourite in an exceptionally critical community. She was tough-minded and communicated it in a style that people were greatly attracted to and responded to with affection and respect. If she indulged people their individual needs, she did not tolerate vulgarity. She believed in propriety, not in the sense of being strait-laced or prissy, but as a check on what could be felt as an imposition of personal idiosyncrasy and as encouragement of self-critical and intelligently detached expression of views. She was not pretty in any conventional sense, and yet her looks were part of her attractiveness. She had a great sense of personal style and used it in her dress, speech and manner to highlight what for other women could have been experienced as unattractive. She was tall and large-boned, and gave an impression of having masculine qualities in her movements, strong face and forthright opinions. When photographed, she preferred her profile, which outlined the unusual cast of her femininity while showing her sharp sense of self-dramatisation and self-parody. In one that could serve as a portrait of any of her urbane, sophisticated heroines, her arms are folded in a relaxed pose exuding order and control, and she looks out in profile with an expression which combines diffidence, confidence and worldliness. Her face is framed by an elaborate mirror or picture frame which is complemented and/or parodied by elaborate necklaces of pearls and beads and a dark dress which is deceptively simple in its expensively architectured cut. The effect is of someone thoroughly enjoying the display of herself while concealing in her highly stylised and mannered composition and tone a very complicated person.

If she was at all unsure of her sexual attractiveness, marriage to Alan Cameron gave her the confidence to grow into a woman who was unafraid of emotional risk.

In her second novel, *The Last September*, she explores the
sexual identity of two young women struggling to figure
out what kinds of women they can become amidst a world
ossified in its sexual conventions and being threatened with
disintegration from within and without. Lois Farquar tries
to escape her moribund home and its traditions by becoming
momentarily attached to a young British soldier on duty in
Ireland in 1920. The relationship cannot come to anything,
not only because it must signify the absurdity of any idea of
stability in Anglo-Ireland of that time, but also because Lois
is frightened of any violation to her fragile sense of herself.
She becomes friends with a woman ten years her senior
who visits the big house and who represents the choice
for women between marriage for stability and a kind of
permanent transience in which her character will remain
untested and latent. In neither case will sexual experimen-
tation or risk become a test of female character as it does for
the author. The same year that she wrote *The Last September*
Elizabeth Bowen also wrote another volume of short stories,
Joining Charles, in which one story in particular explores
the conflict in women of choosing sexual or parental love.
In the title story, a young woman visiting her husband's
parents, worries that their nurturing love is overtaking her
attachment to her husband. Another story in the collection,
'The Jungle', shows how a growing intimacy between two
schoolgirls produces uneasiness which becomes incompre-
hensible misery.

In her fiction Bowen was interested in testing the
formation of female character against the literary and social
traditions which had been responsible for its development.
If she used any of her own life and experience it was to
transform it into an intense but critically detached survey
of the conventions which had created the sense in women
readers of how they might imagine their fates. This certainly
was her own experience, as she reports what the power of
writing meant to her: 'You make a society each time you

write a story. In fact, you are in closer relation to the characters in the story than you will ever be to anyone in real life. It is this ideal relationship of intimacy and power which is to fascinate those who read' (*Why I Write*, 20, 23–24). The differences between the lives of her heroines and her own reflect her critical distance from both her own experience and that of literary character. She acknowledges that 'any fiction . . . is bound to be transposed autobiography . . . I can,and indeed if I would not I still must, relate any and every story I have written to something that happened in my life'. At the same time however, she 'rejects stories which reek' of herself by 'exhibiting sentiments – or betraying them. I am dead against art being self-expression'.[14]

The year after Bowen published *The Last September* and *Joining Charles* her father became ill, going through some of the psychological symptoms he had suffered earlier. He died in May 1930 and was buried in the Farahy churchyard which was part of the original demesne of Bowen's Court. The big house now belonged to Elizabeth and she had to decide how to manage it. The house was not so elaborate as other Anglo-Irish estates and did not have as many rooms; its plumbing dated from Robert Cole Bowen's Victorian improvements. Its attractiveness stemmed from an austerely balanced architecture set against beautiful terrain, all of which were enhanced by Bowen's enthusiastic and energetic hospitality. She entertained constantly when she was there, offering lavish food and drink, provocative conversation, and a penchant for games which her friends enjoyed to the point of inventing or bringing their own. The practical end of things was managed by Alan, who tried his best to relieve the anxiety which persisted in the face of keeping up a house which contributed nothing to its elaborate support. Financial anxiety exacerbated Bowen's ambivalence about a house which had meant prestige and privilege to her male ancestors, but which to her meant attention away from her real vocation and the privilege only nostalgic memory affords. She loved the house for all its turbulent history and trouble, but was never sentimental about it.

Bowen's critical faculties extended to her political life. By the time she wrote the chronicle of *Bowen's Court*, she had clearly formulated her stance in relation to her ancestors' political and cultural history. She never hesitates to point out that what is most seductive in their intense, cultivated style of living is also deadly – destructive to themselves and to those they exploit. In her thirties at a time when many intellectuals in England were being seduced by various ideologies, when Communism and Fascism became the hidden articles of confederation in the clubs of Oxbridge and salons of country houses, Bowen remained aloof. Just as she was on friendly terms with Bloomsbury, but formed her aesthetic in different historical and personal terms, so she resisted the revolutionary thrusts of the political left and right. She preferred to focus on the lives of individuals and to see how they were shaped by their own deployment of ideology, as she does with the character of Robert Kelway in her World War II novel, *The Heat of the Day*.

Her ironic views of the contemporary cultural and political scene led her to begin reviewing for such magazines as *The New Statesman* and *The Tatler*. Consistent with her focus on individual consciousness, her reviews examine the vision and style of the writer before making associations with a literary tradition. It is as though she sees the work of particular writers creating a community only after they are published, rather than seeing them as products of influence. With the publication of *Friends and Relations* in 1931 and *To the North* the next year, her international reputation was established. *Friends and Relations* is the less successful of the two, working against the grain of her focus on individuality. More than any of her fiction, this novel treats domestic ideology at both surface and depth, but the characters' individuality rarely breaks through the convention which

shapes them. *To the North*, by contrast, takes the myths
of domestic happiness and female sexual destructiveness
and tests their assumptions against characters who resist
the expected moves of conventional plots.

The issue of sexuality became a personal one in Bowen's
thirties. She fell in love with Humphry House, a Fellow and
Lecturer in English Literature at Wadham College, Oxford.
He was engaged to be married, but neither this nor Bowen's
marriage deterred either of them from embarking on an
affair of almost overpowering sexual intensity. Although *To
the North* was written two years before the affair began, it
is interesting to note that fears Bowen expressed about the
strengths of her own passion are already present in the affair
of Markie and Emmeline. Like Markie, Humphry House
was taken aback by his lover's powerful desires. The sexual
aspect of the relationship burned itself out, but it had a
profound and lasting effect on Bowen's sense of herself. It is
as though the years of emotional stability and nurturing she
had with Alan Cameron allowed her to grow up so that she
could freely explore that side of her life which had remained
under protective wraps. That she managed to indulge her
passions and keep her marriage on the same satisfactory
plane on which it was founded testifies to the remarkable
balances this woman could exercise amidst complicated and
often conflicting feelings and experiences. Alan never found
out about this affair and if he accommodated himself later
to Bowen's other attachments, it was made possible by the
deep satisfactions each derived from the marriage.

In addition to sexual intensity, the affair taught Bowen
that writing was primary to her life. In a letter Glendinning
quotes from Bowen to her lover, she presents herself as
a character written by herself for herself. Her sense of
audience is repudiated by her 'struggle' for unopposed
self-expression (*VG* 110). She transposes this struggle to
her fiction where her characters yearn to find places for
themselves in worlds where they are or feel like aliens. If

her characters cannot create places where they can thrive emotionally and creatively, she uses them towards her own success. The 'solitary and farouche' child in her own character could become 'relatable' through the creation of her books: 'My writing, I am prepared to think may be a substitute for something I have been born without – a so-called normal relation to society. My books *are* my relation to society' (*Write*, 23).

Bowen's writing does bridge the isolation and silences which she inherited and the world of adult society and literature to which she wanted to belong. By the time she and Alan Cameron moved to Regent's Park, London, in 1935, she had achieved what she wanted. At the time of the move she was waiting for responses to her new novel, *The House in Paris*. Like *To the North*, this work deals with the costs of sexual passion, but here the consequences are played out in league with ambivalence about motherhood. Just as Leopold is trapped by his mother's choices in the past, so she is foiled by the consequences of having desired both sexual passion and motherhood. The novel makes for particularly intense reading in the way it places its characters in a vice of irrational choices. Although they lead to devastation, the choices Bowen gives her characters also express her empathy for their suffering. The vision of fatedness and emotional paralysis is made even more ominous by a sense that history complies with emotional irrationality. Karen's lover Max, Jewish-English-French, is the quintessential outsider, dispossessed. Radiating unrelieved tension and sadness, his very being suggests the forthcoming historic disaster of his time.

In this work Bowen achieves the artistic synthesis of her own aesthetic, moral and emotional obsessions. In her characters' inexorable passions and frustrated desires for power and order one can see resonances of the story of Bowen's Court, which she was to write seven years later. The vision of 'personal life at its most intense' as well as 'fear of dispossession' which made life in the big house obsessive and claustrophobic pervades *The House in Paris* (*BC* 403, 455). Even the patterning of the novel, with its interconnected tripartite structure straining to keep past and present separated, mirrors the feelings of aggression struggling for expression among the characters. The novel is controlled in a way that permits intense emotion to be expressed, but in its elaboration of the nuances and ambivalences of feeling, it keeps the reader deeply involved without assault. It is the most emotionally compelling of Bowen's novels, but for the sake of her artistic integrity and growth, her future work had to take different directions.

The sense of foreboding that she wrote into *The House in Paris* did not infect Bowen's social pace in the years before World War II. She entertained literary and family friends and created an atmosphere which most found irresistible. Those who found her style inhibiting could turn to Alan, who was far more tolerant, particularly of the young women who were dates of the men who were so taken with the celebrated author. Among those who found her friendship supportive and nurturing were the young women writers with whom Bowen identified. The American writers May Sarton and Carson McCullers came to stay in London and at Bowen's Court, encouraged in their writing but sharply rejected in their more intimate advances. With Bowen's growing social and literary influence, Alan seemed to recede. Having suffered eye trouble since he was gassed in World War I, enjoying a challenging and time-consuming career at the BBC, he showed signs of strain amidst the relentless stream of visitors to Clarence Terrace. His drinking increased and he was often short-tempered with the 'Black Hats' who hung about. None of this, however, affected the Camerons' marriage, which had a deep interdependence impervious to outside stress.

Bowen managed commitment and love for Alan along with a life of her own. Throughout the thirties she had several short-lived affairs and none escaped the critical sensibility she brought to her life and her work. Her next novel, *The Death of the Heart*, picks up the theme of intense sociability as a defence against the risks of passion. The self in this work emerges as feeling besieged by a sense of basic incompatibility with the world. The need for stable attachment is played against the equally strong desire to protect oneself from the needs of others. In her own life, Alan's devotion and professional success insulated her from desires which could have assaulted her need for equilibrium. *The Death of the Heart* brought financial success along with critical esteem. A Book Society Choice, it allowed her to do some renovation at Bowen's Court. It also became her most popular novel, its realism and wit accessible to a wide audience. Most recently, it has been dramatised by BBC Television and broadcast internationally.

It was in wartime, however, that Bowen found an atmosphere that was conducive to great emotional and artistic risk. One can see the beginnings in her collection of short stories published in 1941, *Look At All Those Roses*. Combining hallucinatory sensation with a sense of historical realism, stories like 'Attractive Modern Homes' capture a contemporary urban disorientation which prefigures the more dramatic events of the Blitz. During the war Bowen was an ARP warden and served in the Ministry of Information, travelling to Ireland and making reports about Irish attitudes towards England's part in the war. She published a limited edition of a childhood memoir, *Seven Winters*, as well as her great family and cultural chronicle, *Bowen's Court*. She contributed a volume on *English Novelists* to the series on English life and completed her finest collection of short stories, *The Demon Lover*.

For Bowen, the Blitz broke through the polite veneer which had both protected and inhibited experience. It was frightening and exhilarating. She later said: 'I would not have missed being in London throughout the war for anything: it was the most interesting period of my life' (*VG* 158). Perhaps the most profoundly exciting experience of this period was to last the rest of her life. She met Charles Ritchie, a Canadian diplomat, who became her lover and friend. The Anglo-Canadian and Anglo-Irishwoman enjoyed a sense of secret feelings, of living on the sly while in the mainstream of English social and cultural life. He appears as aspects of the character Robert Kelway in the novel *The Heat of the Day*, which is dedicated to him. The fleeting moments of deep attachment which characterise both war and the characters of this novel became the mainstay of Bowen's relationship with Charles Ritchie. They were separated by careers and later his marriage and of course hers, but each found in the other the possibility for fulfilling the passions of being grown-up – interdependent without the primitive dependencies of childhood feelings. In *The Heat of the Day* Stella endures a crisis of self-sufficiency in the face of personal and national betrayal. With full assuredness, Bowen experiments with issues of language and moral abstractions, bringing her heroine to understand the irrevocable ambiguities of adult emotional and moral commitment. Although the novel was a Literary Guild selection, it remains her most difficult, with its unabashed challenges to literary and moral tradition.

The war also brought destruction; her townhouse was hit several times and she and Alan barely escaped being killed. At the end, with victory to celebrate, she was changing her feelings about England. The courage and excitement of the war years gave way to disillusionment about a changing political and social style. As ever critical and unsentimental, Bowen none the less preferred a kind of cultural and intellectual style which, despite their snobberies and lapses, characterised the British educated middle class for her. For this reason and because Alan's health deteriorated, the Camerons spent more time at Bowen's Court than ever before. Making sure that he was cared for, she continued her career, now lecturing abroad and giving radio broadcasts. She was awarded an Honorary D. Litt. from Trinity College, Dublin, in 1949 and wrote a history of the Dublin hotel, *The Shelbourne*.

On 26 August 1952 Alan Cameron died. Her feelings for him are captured in a letter to May Sarton:

> But he's not gone: I feel him so constantly close to me in this house. The chief thing is, not being able to talk. And oh, without him I feel so cold. I think no presence than his can have been warmer.[15]

Bowen expresses her loss in terms she felt throughout her life. Loving presences are felt in their absence in the writer's careful recreation of the places where they resided. Houses which could be cold and silent, haunted by turbulent and destructive family histories, are filled and warmed by memories of close family ties. Bowen's Court, the source of all such houses in Bowen's work, was transformed by the presence of this devoted and nurturing husband who made communication easy. Nevertheless, themes of homelessness and a search for nurturing places were to dominate the remainder of Bowen's life and work. Following Cameron's death, like so many of her characters who lose loved ones, she rarely stayed in one place. She travelled frenetically, lecturing in Europe and the United States, accepting fellowships at American colleges and meeting Charles Ritchie whenever his posts allowed.

Then, in 1960, she suddenly decided to sell Bowen's Court. She realised that her need to retain the impossibly expensive house was out of proportion to her income and was causing her great 'anxiety, the more deep for being repressed, [and which] increasingly slowed down my power to write' (*BC* 458). Although she expected the new owner to move in and make it a family home, he demolished the big house, leaving for her the memory of 'the character of

Bowen's Court . . . in sometimes its silent way, very much alive' (*BC* 459).

In the 1960s Bowen moved around, retracing her life, from Old Headington to Hythe. In these moves she apparently hoped to recapture memories of the warm, supportive relationships she associated with the places where she experienced them. But for every memory or fantasy of maternal love, an experience of maternal abandonment arises, providing a critical check. Thus in her 1954 novel, *A World of Love*, a falling-down big house provides comic relief to the characters' fantasies of romantic love and stability. Even further critical perspective to nostalgic memory is provided by *The Little Girls*, published in 1964. In it three women in their fifties dig up a coffer they had buried as schoolgirls in order to discover the truth about their empty emotional lives. They discover an empty box, symbol of the malice and envy which holds their relationships together. But negativity does not define the last part of Bowen's career. In her last novel, *Eva Trout*, she penetrates the complacent materialism she observed in America and in England in the sixties and early seventies and produces a work that is both angry and comic in tone and technique. Using her deep concern with the crippling effects of silence on character, she explores the meaninglessness of worn-out social conventions and traditions of family life.

In the last years of her life, Bowen found a small cottage on the coast of England near the spot where she had lived with her mother. Plain and unpretentious, it seemed to work against both the grandeur of her ancestral home and the frippery which characterised the villas she shared with her mother. Perhaps because of its simplicity, this last home could be invested with the feelings, memories, and friendships which sustained her through her painful final years fighting cancer. Having divested herself of the encumbrances of her past, she found deep satisfaction in being able to focus on the two things that mattered to her most: her writing and her close relationships. At the time of her death in 1973, she was composing an autobiography as well as the opening of a new novel. A writer to the end, she asked her literary executor to prepare what she had written about her life for publication. Brief as these last pieces are, they express the clearest vision of the places and moments which shaped her life as a writer.

2 *The Last September*

The Last September treats the historical and social forces that shaped Bowen's life and vision. It followed by two years her apprentice novel, *The Hotel*, modelled after Virginia Woolf's *The Voyage Out*, in which a young woman is on vacation among people who are supposedly travelling for fun, but whose interactions expose them as being on the run from the costs of belonging anywhere and to anyone. *The Last September* assesses the constraints of belonging to a land and people from whom it is impossible to escape. This work is set during the Irish Troubles of 1920 at Danielstown, an Anglo-Irish country estate greatly resembling Bowen's Court; the last days of the big house rely on Bowen's appraisal of the Ascendancy. In her view of Bowen family history, the Ascendancy, 'drew [its] power from a situation that shows an inherent wrong. . . . Having obtained their position through an injustice, they enjoyed that position through privilege' (*BC* 453,456). The terrible cost of exploiting the local populace was to be the Irish rebellion that brought disaster to many of the families descended from the original English settlers. Bowen regarded the destruction of the big houses as the inevitable result of entrenched and unchanging attitudes on the part of an unassimilated and exclusive population. As *The Last September* reveals, the Anglo-Irish remained a people who failed to assume direct responsibility for the well-being of that country which suffered the consequences of their self-proclaimed aristocracy.

The subject of the novel is the twilight of Anglo-Ireland and the fate of those younger people born to inherit the myth of the ancestral home. Tied to the demesne by a belief in its power to endow identity and security, 'order and a reason for

26

living', those younger people also suffer its'innate' isolation as well as its 'intense centripetal life' (*BC* 19–20).[1] The big house represents the moral, political and psychological contradictions that shape the Anglo-Irish. Bowen's Court, the inspiration for all such houses, provides a compelling tie to the past as well as traditions and values that were to shape the future. Reading with the hindsight afforded by *The Last September*, we can see the presence of these ties even in *The Hotel*, set so far from Ireland. For despite its comic evocation of a motley and unrelated group of people, *The Hotel* is filled with a wistful yearning for the emotional connection and identity only a family home promises.

Many years after writing *The Last September*, Bowen was to chronicle her own family history which comprises the myth of the ancestral home. She writes of 'the strong rule of [her] family myth . . . A Bowen, in the first place, made Bowen's Court. Since then, with a rather alarming sureness, Bowen's Court has made all the succeeding Bowens' (*BC* 19,32). Describing a stay at Bowen's Court, Bowen reflects how the emotional and political legacy of past inhabitants is felt to be part of its walls and atmosphere. Indeed, the big house seems to haunt and ultimately absorb 'the lives that submerged here' (*BC* 451). In turn, the accumulated perceptions of those who lived at Bowen's Court assume an implicit, sentient power – felt only by those who belong to the estate and tying them to each other, to the past, and to the house in mutually dependent relationships.

Bowen's conception of her family home is reconstituted in the relationship between Danielstown and its residents. This relationship is immutably grounded in her characters' personal and cultural histories, and, consequently, in their feelings about themselves and one another. As the last and female heir to Bowen's Court, she witnessed her father's inability to break free of his own inheritance. Therefore, Bowen is particularly sensitive to the effects of this relationship on one's sense of manhood and womanhood: the men are made to feel impotent by the actual loss of an estate or by the erosion of real political and social power; the women exercise social power only in arranging the seating at dinner. They both come to parody traditional Anglo-Irish expectations of male and female roles. None the less, these people are bound to one another by the pull of the big house, the power of which lies only in the inhabitants' collective memories and fantasies.

It is clear from Bowen's design that the house and the characters serve as metaphors for each other's destinies; in fact, Danielstown is the novel's focus. Through a series of dialogues between the Naylors and their friends, and through the reflections of the characters about themselves and each other, the novel reveals the story of the life and death of Danielstown. Whatever happens to them outside the house, the characters formulate their identities, examine their pasts and speculate about their futures under the influence of those values symbolised in the life and history of the estate.

There are no viable redefinitions of manhood and womanhood in the scenario of Anglo-Ireland. At the centre of Bowen's drama of big house culture is Lois Farquar, the orphaned niece of the estate owner, Sir Richard Naylor. Contemplating the possibilities for her future amidst repressive social conventions and political chaos, she attempts to negotiate a sense of individuality even as she depends on an inbred world clinging precariously to its privilege. The other characters enacting the values and experiences of Anglo-Irish country life foreshadow the meagre possibilities available to those trying to escape. The promises of prestige and power prevent the children of Anglo-Ireland from having a life outside the demesne. For example, Hugo Montmorency's dream of a virile new start in Canada is reduced to the ritual of shaking out his wife's dresses on their country house visits. The dreams of younger characters are also portrayed as self-deceptions. At face value, Livvy Thompson's romance with a British soldier is a comic counterweight to Lois's quest for love and personal expression. The narrator's mocking tone, however, suggests that the role of romantic heroine is a trap for any woman in this novel. A would-be novelist, Laurence understands that his need for self-expression may very well be frustrated. Identifying with Lois's mother, Laura Naylor, Laurence also recognises that rebellion is futile. The mirror image of her friends and relatives, Lois will also discover that her future can only be defined in terms of Danielstown's legacies. Whether she considers a career or marriage, she reflects that 'the unbelievable future became as fixed as the past' (166).

Danielstown embodies a fantasy of limitless nurture and control. Staring 'coldly over its mounting lawns' and dependents, the house has been anthropomorphised by the lives it has absorbed, exactly as Bowen describes Bowen's Court (7). But despite the fact that these are the lives of both men and women, Bowen recreates the house as a symbol of maternal omniscience and omnipotence. Its coldness, remoteness and emptiness, moreover, suggest a decidedly rejecting mother who commits her children to a cruel bind. Represented by Danielstown, Anglo-Ireland is an 'unloving country' whose 'unwilling bosom' threatens to 'smother her children' (66). Yet its inhabitants experience the house as 'a magnet to their dependence' (67). Such visitors as Marda Norton and the Montmorencys endure the awful weather, the desolate insularity and the inevitable rejections offered up at Danielstown along with antique plumbing and lack of electricity because they feel compelled to return to the world that made them.

Lois wavers in the shadow of two dubious legacies: her mother's impulsive rebellion and Danielstown's 'magnetism' (166). Like her mother, she is positioned between two opposing and compelling forces: a man who represents a world outside the big house and secure tradition, and her identification with the house itself:

> And she could not try to explain . . . how after every return – awakening, even, from sleep or preoccupation – she and these home surroundings still further penetrated each other mutually in the discovery of a lack. (166)

Unlike the male characters, who imagine power in the form of running an estate, or, as in the case of Laurence, becoming a writer, the female characters are shown to lack any fantasy not related to the house. It is as though two centuries of being the lady of the demesne has absorbed these women into the very walls. Yet although this identification does not bring personal fulfilment, they continue to yearn.

So complete is the desire to be part of the house's structure, to fuse with the power projected onto it, that the women of Danielstown cannot assess with any detachment the attractions of the external world. It is as though they imagine the house as a human rival to foreign lovers and yet also as lacking satisfaction. How can one otherwise explain a building and a human being 'mutually penetrating each other with a lack'? The language indicates that Lois has confused or conflated home, lover, mother, and herself. Lois's dependence on her home is ultimately unfulfilling because its 'lack' points ironically to its inhabitants' dubious capabilities. Whatever power the house once represented is being destroyed from inside and out. The essential emptiness of people like Mrs Kerr in *The Hotel*, who cannot give Sydney the sense of a loving but non-violating woman on whom to depend for a sense of wholeness, reverberates in the house. The big house reflects what happens to power in women modelled on a tradition of seeing love as a duty to be discharged and life as looking after the 'appropriate' (17). Lois's indecisiveness is the mark of her frustrated attempts to locate her own needs and find a mode of self-expression within an environment capable of both nurturing and letting go. Like her mother, she discovers a dead end. The suffocating bonds of family expectation are ministered by a structure which parodies women's appropriation of patriarchal authority.

Sir Richard and Lady Naylor preside over their cloistered estate and young wards as clients of the house and its traditions. It is Lady Naylor, however, who designs a rule for living that is intensely social, but which excludes all human realities residing between the gates of their demesne and those of other gentry. Despite expressions of sympathy for local families, the Irish are essentially ignored by the Naylors. But not by Bowen. For while they have no plot of their own, indeed, no individualised characterisations, they are implanted in the Naylor's story so that they become the sole agents for change in Anglo-Ireland.

Bowen makes sure that we see the world of Danielstown as victim of its own designs. In all her writing about Ireland Bowen exposes the Anglo-Irish obsession with their homes, an investment necessarily excluding the interests of the outside world and assuring self-absorption. But this does not mean that those in power would have it any other way. Indeed, in order to insure against rivals for that singular, if precarious place in the 'unwilling bosom,' they perform an act of self-justification. They mystify their own power to themselves and to others by creating a myth of the big house as maternal beneficence and benevolence. With each new generation they replicate themselves and the conventions defining their 'intense centripetal life'. The culture of the big house encourages women to identify with the power of this myth. Unfortunately, however, the myth endows them only with the power to enforce conventions which give order to a personal life that in reality reflects the disorders of Anglo-Irish patriarchal politics. Their conventions give both men and women an encoded language by which they communicate only with themselves, about their inherited identities, reinforcing a kind of narcissism born out of loneliness and deprivation, not nurture and love.

Bowen's Anglo-Irish create an artificial world whose only proclaimed inhabitants are themselves. In turn, their political and personal passions have only one object of desire: the estate, which becomes its own island-nation.[2] The compulsion to keep the estate going above all signifies the crippling debt paid to those limestone shrines to the past. According to Bowen, the big house had no future because by 'living for a myth', they refused to 'give history direction' (BC 436,452). The realities denied by the Naylors come home to haunt them in the form they most fear – they are dispossessed. What Bowen refers to as 'keeping the lid on', proves to be a fatal strategy for coping with the threat of imagined or real danger. Ignoring the capture of their Irish neighbours and even the gunfire outside the house, they fall victim to their own blind folly. The world of the Naylors must ultimately burn because 'with a kind of fatedness, a passivity, they resumed the operation of living' (108). Only the invited 'penetrate' Danielstown, so the Naylors think. Conditioned to deny change, their social obligations are transformed into ceremonial acts which celebrate the Ascendancy. Sir Richard worries more about visitors coming down too early for dinner than about his role in Danielstown's destiny. Only his dreams are beset by the political violence threatening his absolute control. Although political matters are not at the forefront of the novel's actions, political implications are embedded in every incident.

Bowen portrays Danielstown as an analogue to its inhabitants' emotional and political blindness, suggesting that the house's apparent omniscience reflects its owners' narcissism. Historically, it has stood only for its own maintenance, ignoring the needs and individuality of its dependents. In turn, its heirs assume that others are

only variations of each other. Thus, Hugo's infatuation
with Marda replays his misperception of Laura Naylor,
the love of his youth. Emblematic of domestic politics
in the big house, he knows nothing about the desires
of his new love or his old except what he needs them
to be. The characters seem imbued with the residual
effects of those qualities ascribed to the house. Francie's
ghost-like presence makes it easy for Danielstown to ignore
her listless attempt to influence Lois, their mutual impasse
reflecting 'the imposingly vacant house' (187). Lois laments
the Naylors' rejection of Gerald Lesworth's unauthorised
warmth: 'You'd think this was the emptiest house in Ireland
– we have no family life' (88). By discouraging free expression of feeling, Danielstown's conventions reinforce 'the
lack' its heirs feel. The women must assume an authority
abrogated by men like Hugo and Sir Richard, and then pay
for it by repressing their own passion and humanity. In the
twilight of this world, both sexes are castrated. Their inbred
system ensures the end of their species. Thus, the big house
also reflects how the narcissism of Anglo-Ireland neuters
its heirs. For its images of 'empty bosom' and castrated
power convey a sense of fused sexual identities adding up
to desexualisation.

The only survivor in this impoverished world is the actual
story of Danielstown. The characters become prisoners to
those traditions upholding the 'family myth'; that is, by
living as though they are replicas of their ancestors, they
transform themselves into figures in an historical romance,
important only to the imagined continuity of the estate.
Before the young even have the chance to live as characters in a more realistic fiction, they are conventionalised,
sacrificing contingency and indeterminacy to the myth of
Danielstown's immortality. Bowen uses the conventions
of realism to promise her heroine an open ending and
self-determination while building a case for the futility
of such a promise. Such a transformation renders the

characters passive, desexualised, and hence incapable of action.

Every character involved with Danielstown is fated to experience struggle with the domination of the past, making any plans for the future, any hope for passion, an exercise in futility or at best, an act of whimsy. Even Marda, whose marriage plans suggest escape from her own transience and the inertia of Anglo-Ireland, assesses herself in relation to Danielstown: 'She might not be fatal, but *here* she was certainly fated' (116). Marda also sees Lois 'pray[ing] for somebody to be fatal' (82). The conventional meaning here indicates that Lois is looking for someone to love, but the use of the word 'fatal' signifies the connection between Lois's feelings and the fatalism enshrouding the big house. The foreboding thoughts ascribed to Lois indeed prove lethal to her suitor, Gerald, who is killed in an Irish Revolutionary Army ambush. Moreover, Lady Naylor's reaction to Gerald's death negates both the value and action of his personal sacrifice by emphasising that the incident was destined: 'he could not help it . . . ' (205). It seems that Anglo-Irish arrogance and ambivalence on the one hand, and the unacknowledged violent fate of Ireland on the other, renders traditional categories of heroism ineffectual. Like its inhabitants, the outsider who dares to set foot inside the demesne is sacrificed to the history of Anglo-Ireland. Gerald is an unacceptable suitor partly because he is English, middle-class and has no money, but primarily because he does not fit the mould of Anglo-Ireland. He is dismissed by Myra Naylor as 'irrelevant,' a rather strange usage, which reduces the soldier protecting her island to a non-person. He is, in effect, treated like the Irish revolutionaries, emasculated by Anglo-Irish commitment to their myth. Those who are more identified with the big house deny yet enact the consequences of Anglo-Irish ambivalence, as Francie's weak heart and Hugo's passivity demonstrate. The sale of Rockriver, his ancestral home, leaves both man and wife free of historic burden, but also denatured – neutered.

Whatever passion went into the conquest of Ireland and the construction of the big houses has ossified into the petty civilities the Naylors and Montmorencys use to perpetuate their ancestors' moral wrongs. Indeed, their generation is but an effete version of their most violent and crude forebears, suffering the 'lack' that haunts Lois. Unlike the Montmorencys, however, who are only ineffectual parents to each other, the Naylors travesty family vitality; they direct their energies towards fashioning Lois and Laurence into sanitised replicas of their forebears. Kept under wraps, the young people are virtually suffocated. Lois muses: 'how is it that in this country that ought to be full of such violent realness there seems nothing for me but clothes and what people say? I might as well be in some kind of cocoon' (49). They are not only unseen, but unheard as well, as Lady Naylor's strategy reveals: 'From all the talk, you might think almost anything was going to happen, but we never listen. I have made it a rule not to talk, either' (26). And later: 'I make it a point of not knowing' (57).

The needs of the younger generation to save their individuality from absorption are regarded as precisely that kind of violence that launched Anglo-Irish identity but now threatens it from within and without. To experience external reality the young must first know how their guardians feel about themselves and the world beyond the demesne. The Naylors succeed in keeping the outside world at bay at a tremendous price to the spirit of those who depend on them. Lois and Laurence do not know how to feel about themselves because the feelings on which identity depends have been deflected into social conventions. Instead of clarifying sexual roles, Anglo-Irish manners and morals only confuse them by making their meaning secret. For the young, life within the house is never experienced directly. The walls themselves appear to reverberate with whispers

and secrets – what people feel but never openly express.[3]
Its dependent children feel as though the 'unavoidable
and containing stare' of the house exposes them, but to
shame, not to knowledge (119). What *is* said comes as a
sinister revelation to those who overhear their lives being
discussed.

The effect of being talked about instead of spoken to,
of overhearing indirectly the determination of one's fate, is
to diminish the sense of a living self. The young are thus
transformed into someone else's fictional creation. When
Lois overhears a conversation about her art school career,
she reacts with anxiety: 'Was she now to be clapped down
under an adjective, to crawl round lifelong inside some
quality like a fly in a tumbler' (60). Indeed, because
Anglo-Irish character is modelled on one's ancestors, the
individual becomes submerged in a rigid pattern. Note how
even the proliferation of names beginning with L mocks this
inbred society: Lois, Laura, Laurence, Livvy, and even the
English Lesworth and Leslie Lawes. Laurence identifies
with Laura's test of self-definition as he views the window
across which she had scratched her name. His association
of this image with that of a wasp 'scrawling Z's on the
air' suggests that like the conventions of this society, the
meaning of one's name as a signifier of sexual identity has
been lost. What it means to rage against such loss is explored
through Laurence's identification with Laura's anguish. He
recalls:

Here, choked in the sweep on the bed curtains, [Laura]
had writhed in those epic rages; against Hugo, against
Richard, against any prospect in life at all; biting the
fat resistant pillows until once she had risen, fluttered
at her reflections, dabbed at her eyes . . . and driven
off, averting from the stare of the house an angry profile.
Hotly, she went up north to attract and marry Mr.
Farquar. It was in her to have done otherwise, but there

is a narrow and fixed compulsion, Laurence recognized, inside the widest ranges of our instability. (107)

Unfortunately for Laura, the wish for violent change disintegrates like her dresses, to 'rot in the attics' (107).

Laurence's language indicates that Laura's rage may have shattered her. Marriage in this world is therefore not an act of self-determination, but another trap of sexual identity. Despite her need for security, Marda also sees marriage as a 'fixed identity' (129). It may seem a relief from the threat of exposure, but marriage only replicates Danielstown's absorption of people by moulding one 'as the bricks and wallpaper of a home' (129). The novel suggests that although marriage does not solve feelings of emptiness, for women, there seem to be no real alternatives. In this novel Bowen characterises love and marriage as an infection innate to Anglo-Ireland – with motherhood the major symptom. Lois observes:

Love . . . was the mainspring of women's grievances. Illnesses all arose from it, the having of children, the illnesses children had; servants also, since the regular practice of love involved a home; by money it was confined, propped and moulded. (60)

Women's illnesses illustrate the 'lack' in Anglo-Irish culture which empowers women to enforce order but renders them powerless to thrive.[4] In *The Last September* two mothers have died. Surely, their absences are part of the emptiness – the lack – Lois feels and fears that a love relationship will duplicate and that she, too, will come to represent. As both Lois and Laurence experience the strong presences of the Naylors as devoid of nurture or support, the lack is exposed as the emblem of the mother and her home who are emptied of life and thus have none to give.

If revolution from the inside is impossible, the longing

for change begins there nevertheless. Laurence's mockery of
Lady Naylor's tactics expresses the anger which results from
passivity. He wishes upon Danielstown the very anarchy its
owners dread in the form that haunted Bowen: 'I should
like . . . some crude intrusion of the actual . . . I should
like to be here when this house burns. . . . And we shall
all be so careful not to notice' (44). Without independence,
language or perceptions, the young cannot even see their
problem to act on it. Dependency thus leads to inertia, a
state which undermines the urge to become an autonomous
individual. Bowen is using adolescence here as a state
of being which is interchangeable with the Anglo-Irish
presence and the subjugation of the Irish. That moment
of transformation from latency to adult sexuality suggests a
suspension between imagining a self and protecting oneself
from annihilation.[5] Lois is trapped between her desire for
an orderly life and her fear of the 'actual' that Laurence
craves. But what is this 'actual' emphasised by its echoed
use? For Laurence it is clearly the political reality which has
underlined Anglo-Irish impotence. For Lois it is the sexual
reality which has turned Anglo-Irish women into ghosts.
Together, Lois and Laurence embody the rage which results
from constraints on their development and which threatens
to break through the language of the Naylors. But while
Laurence may wish for someone else to enact his rage, Lois
fears it entirely. What at first seems to be her awakening
sense of womanhood emerges as the aggression fundamental
to the urge to live. This urge, however, is culturally encoded
as female sexuality which must be repressed and which is
violated before it can ever express aggression. Lois uses
the word '*actual*' (Bowen's emphasis) in response to her
suitor's spontaneous and uninvited arrival at Danielstown
(88). Gerald may be 'ordinary', but what Lois desires and
fears about him endows him with extraordinary power (90).

  Gerald's character embodies the violence done to sexual
identity by the social and political codes of Anglo-Ireland.

His sexuality makes him a real person and hence dangerous, for if his desires are expressed, he has the power to overcome Danielstown's rigid codes. Hence the conflict within Lois's sexual identity is clarified by his presence. She needs Gerald's passion to energise her individuality, but she must also save herself from identifying with his aggression by insulating herself within her home which rejects him.[6] Lois experiences Gerald's kiss as 'an impact, with inside blankness', recalling her feelings about her home and its 'penetration' which 'discovers a lack' (88–89). The similar metaphors signify a fear of being absorbed, by sex or by home, into emptiness and loss of self. The sensation also reaffirms troubled feelings about approaching womanhood which on another occasion she refers to as a 'merciless penetration' (175). Thus, if Lois is not suffocated and lost in sexual union, she may be assaulted by her own emerging aggression and independence. Her antidote against such fears is to imagine sexual love as a sanctuary from feelings of emptiness – a holding environment:

> Lois felt she was home again: safe from deserted rooms, the penetration of silences, rain, homelessness. Nothing mattered: she could have gone to sleep. But he woke her. (150)

The strategies of the narrative associations link this imagined relationship to the very home which promises nurture but which violates the boundaries of selfhood. Thus her awakened sexuality would be as violating as it would be energising. The history of Danielstown has taught her that impotence is the key to survival because sexual energy leads to individual expression which is always anarchic. Bowen's young characters feel that to become individual is to rebel, behaviour which would threaten that very source of nurture necessary to life itself. Therefore Lois must reject Gerald in order for her to submerge her sexual identity within the oppressive security of her family home. In this sense the heroine of *The Last September*, with her ancestral home, is linked to the theme of dispossession. For she is associated with the subjugated Irish who, for generations, have borne their resentment while ekeing out a minimal existence. But where the Irish tenants have been denied the right to create a nurturing place of their own, indeed, have been neutered by real political and economic structures that existed before they were born, Lois is governed by a self-perpetuating myth endowed with power by those who believe in it. What is lacking in the lives of these young characters is ascribed to the big house by becoming, in their minds, another holding environment.

Bowen writes many times of the importance of place as an inspiration, an 'actor', in her fiction.[7] In her autobiographical piece, *Seven Winters*, she reveals how place is an environment created by parents, and then transformed by the child. She describes her parents' marriage as a world which seems to her, in retrospect, to exclude everyone but them:

> I had been born, I see now, into a home at once unique and intensive, gently phenomenal. . . . I find myself writing now of visual rather than social memories. On the whole, it is things and places rather than people that detach themselves from the stuff of my dreams. (11)

Relationships for Bowen become synonymous with places. In her fiction, family life and the family home are characterised as places that fail to communicate feeling and intimacy. In Bowen's life, such isolation led to creativity. For her characters, because no such transformation takes place, we must ask, what happens to feelings which result from experiencing the isolated but claustrophobic family home as a place which suppresses imagination and vitality and is fast becoming an anomaly in times of revolution?

Where is the rage accompanying the loss and castrations Bowen attributes to Lois, to Laura, and to Laurence, but which seems to dissipate within the characters' reveries? Bowen gives her characters no means by which to expiate this rage, and even where it is expressed verbally, it seems to lose its power in the frustrated attempt to transform words into acts.

In two important scenes, however, both taking place away from Danielstown, this rage is suggested by imagery, if not directly by the characters. Rage and rebellion are enacted in the mill scene, away from Danielstown, involving Hugo, Lois and Marda, but leaving them on the periphery of the action which precipitates and enacts anarchic feeling. The event becomes central to the novel's meaning precisely because it indicates how the characters of the big house may be 'superfluous' to the political realities of Ireland and to the expression of feeling within the novel. Indeed, the 'dead' mill is a sinister version of the place symbolising Anglo-Ireland's 'lack': 'the house of Usher's . . . like corpses at their most horrible . . . another . . . of our national grievances' (123,124). These references connect cultural, political and sexual deprivation. Ireland may be a country full of decayed monuments to Irish powerlessness and to the lifeless domination of the Anglo-Irish, but such quiescence is deceptive. Entering the mill, Marda and Lois surprise a sleeping rebel, who brandishes a pistol. The fact that the pistol is fired by accident and not dramatised calls attention to the impotence of both rebel and witnesses. But the mill scene suggests that violence is embedded in the novel, even if no one seems capable of committing it. By observing the event and not participating in it, Lois and Marda repeat the historic role of women in Anglo-Ireland. As the rebel warns them, they 'better . . . keep within the house y'have it' (125). As hostesses of 'the democracy of ghostliness', they, too, may become spectral, equivalent to 'broken palaces in futility and sadness' (123).

Lois's confrontation with external reality reveals that even rebellion duplicates the methods of the oppressor. Keeping the Irishman's presence a secret is an attempt to discover and preserve a reality that Danielstown conceals from Lois and Marda. The two women safeguard it from becoming a conventional fiction, victim of the need to censor a story foretelling the violent end of the big house and the transformation of its women into ghosts. In this way Lois's secret is an untold story, but as with any well-guarded secret, its impact dies with suppression. Thus, neither Lois nor Marda can be rebels. Lois's only outlet for autonomy is to usurp Danielstown's method of suppression and reconstitute it. She turns the event into an expression of feeling that she and Marda can share in an intimate, if somewhat cool and transient, relationship. The combination of women's mutual understanding and mistrust harks back to *The Hotel*, where Sydney only experiences authentic feeling with a woman who represents 'the good/bad godmother' (*VG* 67). Just as Lois rejects Gerald, Sydney breaks her engagement with one man and rejects another, situating her desire for intimacy in her relationship with Mrs Kerr. In all of her fiction, Bowen will explore how women's lack of self-sufficiency makes them ambivalent about relating to each other. As co-conspirators, keeping themselves alive by preserving their cultural myths, they must keep any 'lack' a secret. Such a strategy, highlighting the self-destructiveness of such myths, is part of the continuum of female relationships from *The Hotel* to *Eva Trout*, her last novel.

The barracks dance, like the mill scene, illustrates radical disjunctions between moral and emotional life, between traditional gender roles and the imperatives of individual desire. Bowen identified these disjunctions in the Ireland of her childhood and wove them throughout her later fiction. A pivotal figure in Bowen's development of female character, Lois faces her own struggle between passivity and aggression in an encounter with a man who is disintegrating under the weight of the moral bankruptcy around him. Daventry, a British officer and the counter-weight to the Irish rebel in the mill, is an outsider in Ireland. He, too, is sinister but psychically wounded, in this case by orders to brandish power of dubious value: ransacking beds for guns in 'houses where men were absent and old women or women with babies wept loudly and prayed' (144). The scene establishes a tension between the sexual energy generated by the dance and the impotence Daventry, Lois and Gerald feel. Lois and Daventry also experience a brief moment of recognition, but only to reinforce their mutual sense of displacement, dehumanisation and powerlessness. While Daventry's job requires him to participate in the rape of Ireland, Lois and Gerald lose their sexual impetus. As the characters retreat from each other, passion and rage are expressed only through the spontaneous explosion of objects. Balloons explode, a gramophone is upset, and a room throbs as though it would burst.

The juxtaposition of incapacitated people and energised objects, however, is not comic, as one might expect. It suggests instead an absurd and horrifying relationship between the inability to feel and the eruption of violence. The echoes here of the mill scene thus establish a link between the repression of violence and of responsibility. Those whose feeling is preserved in an object – the big house – literally sit around or disappear from the novel while their country explodes around them. The separation of concealed rage from the outbreak of aggression necessary to live shapes the novel's violent ending while revealing Bowen's ambivalence about her ancestral home.

In her essay 'The Big House' Bowen expresses reverence for the comforting forms of gracious living which aestheticise an otherwise gloomy and precarious existence (*BH* 197–199). In *The Last September*, however, such justification breaks down. After all, for Lois, as for her

mother, those very traditions also require 'the subjugation
of the personal to the impersonal. In the interest of good
manners and good behaviour, people learned to subdue
their feelings' (*BH* 199). Twenty-five years after writing
The Last September Bowen admits that such a strategy might
also have been 'foolhardy or inhuman'. Lois's 'acquiescence
to strife, abnormalities and danger', deflects what she might
feel toward the family and home which not only fail to
nurture her, but threaten to incorporate her into a vision of
desexualised but insidiously aggressive womanhood (*P* 98).
The portrait of Lois may have been a means of diffusing
the powerful emotions which bound Bowen to her heroine
and to the big house. For as Bowen admits: 'This, which
of all my books is nearest my heart, has a deep, unclouded
spontaneous source. . . . It is a work of instinct, rather
than knowledge' (*P* 96). Examining her work in retrospect,
Bowen appears uneasy about Lois's indifference to 'the
national struggle around her' (*P* 98). The response may
describe her own reaction as well as that of her heroine. 'In
part, would not this be self-defence?' (*P* 99). At the time
Bowen wrote the novel, she apparently felt a strong need to
distance herself from her heroine and to keep Danielstown
discrete from Bowen's Court. As a 'niece always, never
child of that house', Lois cannot feel the full emotional and
economic impact of the big house as her creator did (*P* 99).
When word is received of Danielstown's destruction, there
is no indication of Lois's reaction, for in keeping with the
open ending, the heroine has departed from the pages of
the book.

With twenty-five years of distance, Bowen wonders if
it was 'sorrow to [Lois], Danielstown's burning?' (*P* 99).
One supposes that Bowen is asking about her own reaction
if Bowen's Court had burned. Although it was spared,
destruction was a grim possibility that haunted Bowen
during those difficult years. She describes the feelings
that compelled her to write *The Last September* later:

I *was* the child of the house from which Danielstown derives. Bowen's Court survived – nevertheless, so often in my mind's eye did I see it burning that the terrible last event in *The Last September* is more real than anything I have lived through. (*P* 100)

Bowen's ambivalence about the big house is divided between the pain of imagining her family home in flames and the wish to be free of its burdens and constraints.

In the novel's conclusion, Bowen both expresses and deflects her conflicted feelings. While the heroine and her friends leave the stage of war and the Naylors suffer in appropriate silence, the writer, with the help of Irish rebels, sets fire to the big house. Again, the object bears the brunt of human feeling, but here people alien to the demesne are responsible for its explosion. The language describing the conflagration testifies to the strange relationship between the house and its inhabitants:

A fearful scarlet ate up the hard spring darkness; indeed, it seemed that an extra day, unreckoned, had come to abortive birth that these things might happen. It seemed, looking from east to west at the sky tall with scarlet, that the country itself was burning . . . The roads in unnatural dusk ran dark with movement, secretive or terrified; not a tree, brushed pale by wind from the flames, not a cabin pressed in despair to the bosom of night, not a gate too starkly visible but had its place in the design or order and panic. At Danielstown, half way up the avenue under the beeches, the thin iron gate twanged (missed its latch, remained swinging aghast) as the last unlit car slid out with the executioners bland from accomplished duty. . . . Then the first wave of a silence that was to be ultimate flowed back confidently to the steps. The door stood open hospitable upon a furnace. (206)

The 'open and empty country' burning against a 'bosom of night' reinforces Bowen's extended metaphor of the big house representing Anglo-Ireland as a rejecting, castrating and controlling mother who now suffers poetic justice.

Devoid of nurture, compassion or stability, the house is appropriately gutted. It is as though enraged children reciprocate her maternal favours by eating up the house that threatened to eat them. Thus, they deliver an 'abortive birth' to the myth of Danielstown's continuity, committing its rejecting door to infinite 'hospitality'. But Bowen also shows the injustice of such poetic symmetry in her metaphor. If the maternal object has become omnivorous, it is because women have no *raison d'être* beyond maintaining the only traditions available to them. If these traditions have left the men emasculated, clinging to powers they mostly dissipated, the women have no choice but to assume patriarchal responsibilities. The consequences in political and social terms are a matter of record. What Bowen accomplishes is to link those consequences to the cost of human sexual identity. For castrated men and women are not only sterile, but disappear in their interchangeability.

The Irish who rebel against oppressive landlords express the rage of the big house characters. They are the instruments of action and feeling which Bowen shows are denied Lois, Laura and Laurence by the moribund dream of the Ascendancy. The novel implies that the relation between the Irish and the big house is also that of deprived, castrated and oppressed children and controlling and indifferent parents. The Irish fulfil Laurence's wish and burn the cocoon, freeing the children of the Ascendancy to realise their own capacity for life. But although Danielstown is destroyed, the myth of the ancestral home thrives in the wishes, needs and fantasies of Bowen's characters in future novels. Even in those works set far from Ireland, characters desperately yearn for the power, identity and sense of purpose which they associate with belonging to a family home.

With *The Last September* Bowen became a successful novelist, exploring characters who desire the nurturing promise of a family home, but who experience its overwhelming demands instead. Having left her ancestral home herself, Bowen found the answer to professional identity in England. Nevertheless Ireland, with its memories of her Anglo-Irish childhood and historic roots, remained for her a private retreat and the place where she continued to search for the source of her creative energy. Regardless of the setting of her subsequent work, Bowen is never far in her imagination from the world she knew so well and described so evocatively in *The Last September*.

3 *Friends and Relations* and *To the North*

Following her creative breakthrough in *The Last September*, Bowen wrote *Friends and Relations*. Moving away from an obviously autobiographical subject, Bowen says in fact that 'it was England that made me a novelist'.[1] Leaving behind the emotionally charged context of her family history, she devotes her creative energies in her third novel to a subject which seems to make no personal claims on her. The time-honoured constraints of the Anglo-Irish big house are replaced here by the flux of changing English values.[2] Following a convention used by George Eliot in *Middlemarch* and later transformed by D. H. Lawrence in *Women in Love*, Bowen begins her novel with a wedding in an idyllic country setting. The nuptials of Laurel Studdart and Edward Tilney occupy a middle ground between Eliot's view of social change amidst relative stability and Lawrence's apocalyptic view of a world destined for self-destruction. This English tradition provides the context for Bowen's primary concerns: the house as province and metaphor of woman's condition and family relations is now extended to highlight the character of the mother as the bulwark of the family home.

In *Friends and Relations* a nostalgic yearning for family life is undercut by a graphic portrayal of family instability. As in Henry James, personal desire is ultimately renounced, but Bowen sees the moral destiny of the family as the central problem. The power of the past, which in *The Last September* was represented by aristocratic values, is presented in this new work as the personal desires of a woman. Despite the optimism conveyed by the

Studdart-Tilney marriage, the disturbing past of Lady
Elfrida Tilney haunts and threatens the younger generation's chances for happiness and stability. Edward's
mother, the key figure in this story of marital betrayal,
left her family some twenty years earlier for Considine
Meggatt, a wealthy landowner and sometime big game
hunter. Lady Elfrida's presence unsettles the present,
giving this moral drama an acute psychological edge
and sense of destiny in which both male and female
characters feel their sexual identity is mirrored. Lady
Elfrida and her story precipitate the crisis on which the
plot, the chronology, and the characters' lives hinge. All
of the romantic and family tensions in the novel are tied to
the potentially controlling past of Elfrida's story. Bowen's
drama of repressed passion shows how the stability of
family life and of a class she was to describe later as
'having changed the least', was threatened all along from
within.[3]

The dominant but enigmatic presence of Lady Elfrida
foreshadows the sexual doubts and fears that beset so
many of the characters. Present or absent, Elfrida serves
as a model by which the other women measure their own
needs and moral character and through which Elfrida's son
may feel himself to be a man. Bowen shows how adult
relations in a domestic novel are compelled by expectations
and betrayals between mothers and children. Highlighting
Edward's feelings are the needs and destinies of several
child characters. Whenever they appear, Anna and Simon
Tilney and Hermione Meggatt refocus the limelight away
from their parents and onto the mother–child symbiosis that
both informs and defeats adult passion. Hermione pleads
with her mother to 'go on holding me tight, don't go; I
wish we were the same person' (110). On the morning after
Edward has disappeared, his daughter Anna comforts her
mother in a way that is unmistakably maternal. In each
case the child becomes Bowen's reminder of how mothers

are cast as emotional and moral barometers of the family's stability and how they are made responsible for the character of the child.

Whatever power is attributed to the attraction between Edward and Janet, the drive to act derives more from Janet's perception of herself as mother and from Edward's character as his mother's child. When Edward comes to Batts Abbey to retrieve his children from the corrupting presence of the elderly ex-lovers, his mother and Considine, his sense of moral purpose is defeated by feelings he cannot control. The passion which underlies Edward's quarrel with Janet seems orchestrated by the memory of Elfrida's adultery. In a confrontation requiring either parental responsibility or adult sexuality, Bowen shifts the ground of the domestic novel to the passion of children. Edward's 'dread and desire' for Janet conflate the danger of a mother's sexuality and the childhood damage from which he still suffers (95). His 'mounting excitement under [Janet's] manner, [for] penetration' is deflated by imagining that 'he was Janet' (95).

The language here suggests that Edward's fear of being 'fused' with Janet is threatening to his character (95). Edward's passion identifies male with female character, upsetting the distinct cultural ordering of gender as it has traditionally been represented in the domestic novel. Bowen shows how domestic order is disturbed by a male sexuality formed in defence of its own persistent image of woman as all-powerful mother. As a mother of young children who is contemplating an adulterous affair, Janet is a potential version of Elfrida. This doubling is reinforced by their mutual and exclusive understanding. Janet tells the older woman: '*You* were the reason I married Rodney. . . . I wanted to be related' (105,106).

The strong sexual feeling of both women represents 'cold, dispassionate passion' to men (36). Hence Janet's passion for Edward is expressed as a will to dominate.

Years before, she thinks: 'I could hold you, yes, and make you run about, in the palm of my hand' (36). The fate to which Elfrida subjects Considine is the consequence of such a will, as the discarded lover himself testifies:

> Her silence . . . had been a wound for him . . . She undid passion. . . . [H]e left behind with her in that apartment, where she had created . . . an icy but very real hearth, the whole spring of his being, a manhood she had demanded then undone. (68)

Considine's unmanning prefigures the decline and death of Edward's father, which along with the son's stunted sexual identity, indicts Elfrida as the prototypical ice maiden, inciting passion in others while precipitating a kind of 'overruling disorder' (104). Generalising about the breakdown of family morality, the narrator infers cosmic implications from the behaviour of both Elfrida and Janet:

> Today proved to be one of those weekdays, vacant, utterly without character, when some moral fort of a lifetime is abandoned calmly, almost idly, without the slightest assault from circumstances. So religions are changed, celibacy relinquished, marriages broken up or there occurs a first large breach with personal honour. (69)

The damage suggested here by broken homes occurs in a way that is particularly significant for Bowen. Elfrida's desertion is recalled as occurring 'without any explanation', but with the result that Edward loses his home (24). So Bowen recalls her father's internment when she 'left Herbert Place forever, without knowing' (*BC* 417). The memory of her mother's illness is equally disturbing, as it 'was kept a mystery from [her]' with talk her parents knew 'to be fictions' (*BC* 423). The price paid for these mystified events is one Bowen knew to be devastating. Edward becomes 'unintelligible', a symptom revealing his helpless rage toward the abandoning mother he cannot forgive (17). In so much of Bowen's fiction, when children lose their mothers, they lose their capacity for self-expression. Like Lois and Laurence in *The Last September*, Eva Trout and her mute son, Jeremy, in Bowen's last novel, have no mother they can rely upon, no language of self-expression, and never figure out their reason for being. Whether or not Jeremy blames his adopted mother for her inability to fulfil his needs, he certainly expresses rage as he shoots her fatally at the end. In each instance Bowen sympathises openly with the damaged child, but more indirectly problematises the traditional portrait of betraying mother.

Abandoning the child may be the last straw for a woman whose only recourse to autonomy has been to retreat into sexual passion or into herself, 'distraite . . . like a ghost rumoured, perhaps seen' (85, 70). Portraying Elfrida as beyond renunciation or redemption, Bowen dramatises a woman's struggle to negotiate her sexual identity outside of motherhood and sexual passion. As it takes place within the novel's intricate patterning, submerged in the texture of its realistic surface, this negotiation reflects Bowen's understanding of the impact of literary conventions in the English novel on the formation of female character. Like the passion and even the childlessness of Bertha Mason in *Jane Eyre*, both of which are facets of her self-definition hidden in her husband's gothic attic, moral dramas hide and then reflect women's repression of personal desire. Within the pattern of making Elfrida and Janet doubles in a drama of family morality is embedded the fear that beyond sexual passion and motherhood there is nothing, only, as Janet tells Edward, in rejecting him, his mother's 'spent . . . life' (134). If Janet's decision protects Edward by affirming maternal responsibility, it leaves the question of a woman's restlessness open: 'She herself still lived and had to command emotion: Elfrida and Considine seemed to have died young' (74).

Rejected by Janet, Edward goes back to Laurel, whose unequivocal devotion makes her the ideal wife and mother. Our response to Laurel, however, as to Elfrida's and Janet's characterisations, is directed ultimately by the anger and aggression of a younger woman, Theodora Thirdman, the prototype of Bowen's untamed adolescent. Unlike the tormented characters in *The Last September*, she is not helpless. Witness to all the action, she is also no mere innocent bystander. She is a child spying on betraying adults, promising a 'wild kind of justice' as she engineers both the mother's punishment and her unwavering closeness (78). An outsider, unwanted, Theodora forces connections by writing a letter which brings on the novel's crisis. Avenging herself on a world of betraying parents, she exposes all their hidden passions, and in so doing, her own. Of course, Bowen always believed that writing is a powerful instrument of self-expression. It enables the child to 'approximate to [her] elders, yet to demolish them'.[4] She wrote in her response to V. S. Pritchett's *Why I Write*:

> Perhaps one emotional reason why one may write is the need to work off, out of the system, the sense of being solitary and farouche. Solitary and farouche people don't have relationships: they are quite unrelatable. If you and I were capable of being altogether house-trained and made jolly, we should be nicer people, but not writers. . . . (23)

Writing in this novel wrests events away from 'tragic coincidences' and gives the enraged child control (40). Theodora's letter prepares the reconciliation of the two marriages, making the farouche child a powerful *deus ex machina* who arranges events so that parents fulfil her frustrated needs.

Underlying the domesticated resolution at the novel's end remains a 'disturbance', however, a 'mislaid pattern', indicating disjunctions between maternal responsibility, childhood needs, and the desires of the mother (156,157). The pattern implies that because the child's needs for nurture and stability are insatiable, the family's inability to fulfil them is perceived as betrayal. Maternal responsibility reminds women that while their best efforts will always fall short of the symbiosis craved by children, the world of the family neither nurtures the mother nor allows her any options for fulfilment outside its domain/demesne. Bowen embeds the question of alternatives for women in the voice of a character presented as the bulwark of the family. In the denouement Laurel's mother expresses anxiety about her daughter's self-sacrifice: 'I wish there were something else she could be, not a woman . . . *I can't bear life for her!*' (158, Bowen's italics). The wish remains rhetorical until we consider Theodora's fate. A lesbian, Theodora's passions will preclude motherhood. If she has a profession, it remains 'above discussion' (59). Given her outsize character, she is capable of encompassing not only the demands of children but the inexpressible desires of womanhood. Her rage provides the outlet for creative and sexual energies, shaking up and resettling family life while saving herself from it. Bowen's alleged conservatism about women's roles is thus only one side of her story. The significance she attaches to maternal presences and absences in family homes becomes a staple of her writing, expressing empathy for children's needs while carefully embedding the issue of women's desires outside motherhood.[5] For Bowen, women's sense of self is always an undeclared war on the view that their sexuality is dangerous and is best channelled and defused by maternal responsibility. That Elfrida's sexuality is threatening to her lovers and son is cogently linked to her lack of desire to be either a wife or a mother. If *Friends and Relations* spreads the implications of this link over all its female characters, her next novel will compress it into one.

Almost without exception, critics have agreed that Elizabeth Bowen's *To the North* works 'close to the world of fairy tales', playing out a melodrama of innocence betrayed by a 'satanic' cad.[6] This design enables Bowen to explore the implications of a tradition of female sexual danger that she plotted in *Friends and Relations*.[7] This form is established in the melodramatic romance between Emmeline Summers and Markie Linkwater. After a whirlwind courtship, Markie reverts to his pursuit of other women and Emmeline is left betrayed and wanting. Neither sermon nor soap opera, however, fits the complex of values and feeling created by the narrative design. Within this moral fable is a story more closely related to myth. The portrayal of Emmeline as 'glacial' angel foretells her metamorphosis into a goddess of death (14–15). As in myths of Medea and Clytemnestra, her metamorphosis enacts a drama in which a woman's unleashed sexual passion inevitably becomes an instrument of death. Although killing herself and her lover are precipitated by his betrayal, Emmeline's potential for violence is endemic to her sexuality. From the very outset, without provocation, Emmeline, like her ancient prototypes, impresses her lover as both desirable and terrible. Reinforcing its mythic sense, the narrator holds Emmeline's character responsible for the shape and substance of the novel's events:

> Innocence walks with violence; violence is innocent, cold as fate; between the mistress' kiss and the blade's is a hair breadth only, and no disparity; every door leads to death. . . . The curtain comes down, the book closes . . . (185)

In this novel Bowen moves away from the embedded patterning of *Friends and Relations* to a method more dramatically ironic. She creates a narrator who is coldly distanced from womankind. In fact, the narrator's olympian tone and stance pronounce judgements which mimic all those myths which represent woman as sexually destructive. The mythic mode, however, enlarges the perspective. As the passage above shows, by conflating such contrasting abstractions as innocence and violence and equating them with a woman's lethal sexuality, this generalised characterisation also comes to resemble a figure in psychological fantasy or in a dream.[8] The function of this fantasy in the novel's structure shows that Bowen does not intend the mythic dimensions of Emmeline's character to be the final judgement, but only the dramatisation of a dominant perception of women. For the conflation of innocence and sexual destructiveness draws attention to man's paradoxical desire and fear of the woman who must, to his satisfaction, prove to be dangerous after she beguiles him with her innocence. Bowen portrays this universal theme in the fantasies of Emmeline's lover, Markie. She then undercuts this view by showing that there is a very different story to tell. The sense of universal truth conveyed by the rhetoric of anthropomorphised abstractions and by the specific fears of one man is set against Emmeline's fantasies. In turn, the unique desires and fears of one woman structure a rejoinder to myths about women. Recognising the mythic counterparts to Bowen's portrayal of women enables us to read this novel as a gloss on the ideological assumptions which women writers must combat in order to create their own female characters.

Bowen's response to myths about women's sexuality takes on the one thematic paradigm that recurs across time and place: the power of female sexuality.[9] The persistence of this theme is matched by a prevalent method of characterising women: splitting them into images of 'angel' and 'monster'. If we see the relationship between this theme and its typical characterisation as a story of fear, its popularity is understandable. In Greek mythology, a model of ingenious variation for western literature, the split between nurturing Demeter and erotic Aphrodite or between the passive Iphegenia and the defiant Antigone creates easily recognisable categories of passive woman-good and defiant-bad. Such a narrative strategy separates nurturing qualities, evaluated as innocence, from erotic sexual desire, judged as aggression.[10] The prototype of nurturing innocence is, of course, the madonna, whose sexuality is defined purely as giving life to and grieving over the loss of her son. Denying women any drive other than mothering reveals that a woman's ability to give life is by itself too powerful to be imagined as aggressive or perhaps not entirely benign and beneficent by itself.[11] Splitting the whole woman in this way defends against a mythic vision of women overpowering the earth named after their fecundity and therefore implies that the presence of sexual desire, aggression and nurture in one woman is dangerous and therefore unimaginable.

To the North reveals Bowen's concern with the implications of this undying tradition of which she is a part. For when a woman is portrayed as an innocent *ingenue* in an English novel, she is already invested with the sexual ideology it has adopted from classical and religious mythology. In order for Dickens' Esther Summerson to remain innocent, she must be maternal, and her disfigurement prevents her from ever being perceived solely as sexually alluring, despite her happy marriage. The tradition in which Bowen works, including Richardson's Pamela and Clarissa, Maria Edgeworth's Belinda, Eliot's Gwendolyn Harleth, and Lawrence's Brangwen sisters, insists that no matter how sheltered and innocent a young woman may be, the moment she strives for self-definition outside this split, her sexuality becomes both alluring and treacherous. The actions of Emmeline Summers would seem to fulfil men's fears, but Bowen's narrative structure and voice and an intricate pattern of imagery revise the traditional tale of fallen innocence. They show how a woman is driven to use her sexuality as an instrument of power because she possesses no other.

The intensity of feeling resonating through the romance of Markie and Emmeline is relieved and glossed by a domestic comedy of manners in which the character of Emmeline's sister-in-law, Cecilia Summers, demystifies the lovers' relationship. Cool and controlled, Cecilia is not only Bowen's witty counterthrust to the myth of women's sexual volatility, but a foil by which we are made to see through man's phobia. Cecilia exposes the purpose of those myths which domesticate dangerous women. The narrator joins forces with Cecilia to view Markie as 'satanic and malevolent', a 'tomcat' and 'voluptuary' – in short, the quintessential bounder (7,104,149). This judgement, however, is modified by Cecilia's bemused response to him. To her he is more an 'agreeable reptile', a man who works hard to protect his appearance of 'importance' (7,9). Cecilia's cynicism reveals the vulnerability lurking behind Markie's posture. Working against the grain of a stock figure, Bowen depicts the cad as disguising his innate dread of being involved with women. In one sense Emmeline is simply the realisation of this dread. In another, she represents the history and destiny of women who are powerless to counteract that dread in others.

Cecilia's 'mistrust' gives critical perspective to the story of Markie and Emmeline, but it also serves as a smoke-screen, concealing and explaining away the disturbing intensity of the lovers' feelings. The weight of prophetic dream conveyed by these feelings not only shifts the narrative from realistic to mythic plot, but suggests the obsessive quality of fantasy against which realistic, mythic and melodramatic plots prove poor defences. Both drawn to and threatened by each other, Emmeline and Markie compel the novel's interlocking narratives to the finish – until 'the curtain comes down' – because their worst fears are irrepressibly enacted by their greatest desires.

Despite the complexity of Emmeline's character, its contradictions can easily be attributed to the moral dimensions of her short-circuited sense of reality. A successful travel agent and presumably independent, Emmeline none the less lives in a world of protective shadows. Her myopia and failure to wear her glasses signify her conflict between 'longing to break the mirror and touch the earth' and her wish to see and touch the world only as she imagines and idealises it (106). But her blindness, which allows more things to happen to her than she controls, permits the emergence of another side of her character. The way she yields to a sense of inevitability parallels a mythic sense of metamorphosis or a psychological sense of non-rational compulsion. In either case, her myopia points to the artistic and ideological origins of her mythic character. Emmeline's blindness contributes to a picture of 'unborn', indeed sexless and childlike womanhood, encouraging belief in her innocence but also preparing for the emergence of her danger (107). Although Emmeline resists Markie's 'incapacity to be satisfied', his 'ravages on serenity', she is finally swept away by the sense of power it gives her (145). At first assaulted by her own awakening sexuality, 'feeling, clawed like a bear', she then feels 'winged like an angel' (125).

Markie is a willing partner, but only to a point. On the surface, his attraction to Emmeline seems like a sardonic comment on the conventional masculine challenge to conquer the elusive *ingénue*. But like Emmeline, his blindness to the danger in his desire makes him prey to other forces. In providing the props for the birth of Emmeline's impassioned character, Markie's 'theatre' of seduction also sets the stage for his unmanning (71). 'Under the fairly imposing surface of his masculinity', his vulnerability is exposed in his plea: 'For God's sake, be kind to me' (145,138). But once Emmeline's sexuality is released, it takes on a life of its own, discarding all control and overwhelming her lover: 'She was embarked, they were embarked together, no stop was possible; she could now turn back only by some unforeseen and violent deflection . . . ' (138).

The fatalistic sense of the lovers' dangerous and 'set course' is heightened by the representation of violent emotions that develop between them. Bowen portrays their feelings as so powerful as to be determining forces locked in battle outside them (138). The lovers' cryptic language is clarified only by an elaborate pattern of imagery and the narrator's gloss. Because it is removed from the characters' consciousness, the affective power of the imagery also has a life of its own, directing the narrative design, the formation of character, and ultimately the reader's response. Because it is controlled by a force unknown to the characters, this emotive power denies them conscious choice in two ways. Unable to articulate their own feelings, the lovers seem to be victims both of their own unconscious needs and of a myth whose narrative forms cast them in preordained roles, speak for them, and interpret their actions.

Leaving the drama to the interplay between imagery and narrative voice affects the reader as well. The circumspect expression of sexual feeling, both on the part of the narrative voice and the characters, is probably what has led most readers to overlook the fantasies embedded in the imagery. But the language effects a rhetorical strategy which not only disarms readers, but provides an exegetical prompt; it revises the myth Bowen recounts by revealing the lovers' fantasies about each other. One such fantasy, about the lovers' first night together in Paris, is presented as Markie's consciousness but interpreted by the narrator. In an otherwise innocuous scene where he awaits her descent in an elevator, we learn the point to Markie's earlier plea:

> Travelling at high velocity he had struck something –
> her absence – head on, and was not so much shattered
> as in a dull recoil. . . . for he had been oppressed since
> last night by sensations of having been overshot, of
> having, in some final soaring flight of her exaltation,
> been outdistanced . . . (142)

Neither Markie nor Emmeline is given words for this
experience; only the narrator has the power to articulate
their fantasies. But since the narrator's interpretation locates
Markie's response 'since' or after his fateful encounter with
Emmeline, the reader must reattach the imagery to the
lovers' sexual experience in order to assess its impact.
In such a reading, the narrator's language insists that
what occurs between Emmeline and Markie is a life and
death struggle, not simply a sad tale of a jilted innocent.
Although Emmeline is depicted as wishing to be submissive
and gentle, she is made to beat her lover at his own game.
Her sexuality has 'sent her a good way past him' so that
later Markie comes to fear for his very manhood and for
his life (142):

> He had a frightening glimpse – as she stood serious,
> eyeing him . . . of how very high a structure there
> was to come down. The tall tower, that rocked by
> some shock at its base or some flaw in its structure
> totters and snaps in the air, falls wide; the damage is
> far-flung; you cannot stand back enough, it is upon you.
> Markie, in whom something cowered, was much afraid
> for himself. He was afraid, as she stood there so gently
> beside him, as much *of* as for Emmeline: it was almost
> physical . . . (184)

Conflating past and present tenses, the narrator articu-
lates what Markie can only intuit and Emmeline can

only enact – a fantasy so physically and psychologically violent, so persistent, that it must be considered the central motive in Markie's abandonment of his lover. He experiences Emmeline in two horrifying forms: as a force so volatile and so unconscious of her inherent danger that it renders him helpless and passive. Appearing to him as a 'tower' of 'Alpine height', the vision threatens to castrate and annihilate him (183). Yet the fact that he returns to Emmeline even after experiencing her as phallic woman suggests that he is attracted to precisely what he fears. The lovers' danger to each other, however, is only apparent in the imagery which embodies the fears and desires of Emmeline and Markie. Strong as the language is, its expression through the narrator's voice deflects attention away from the characters whose experience it describes, inviting abstract, metaphysical interpretation.

If Markie's fantasies have any credibility in the novel's total design, Emmeline must be viewed as a monster, not unlike those goddesses of ancient and classical mythology – a Medusa or Circe and certainly a more graphic version of a young Lady Elfrida. Such a vision, combined with Markie's return to Emmeline, expresses a need and dread of the woman whose power to affirm manhood may also mean the power to cast doubt, or worse, to destroy. If Markie is doomed to be destroyed by this sexual monster, surely he is a victim. But consistent with Bowen's revision of myth, we are given no reason to sympathise with Markie. In the light of his characterisation, even empathy is dissuaded. Although Markie's fantasies form the core of his character, because they conform to universal patterns of sexual fear, they do not distinguish him as an individual. But their connection to mythic patterns undermines the reader's empathy as well. For unlike Jason or Agamemnon, Markie is no hero. The evidence for this surfaces early when Emmeline's penchant for fast cars and planes contrasts with Markie's inability to drive and later when he admits that he 'can't live at top gear'

(183). Combined with his inability to sustain the emotional level of his fantasied desire, his fear of high speeds cuts him down with ridicule. Furthermore, whatever we see of his consciousness is made irremediably unsavoury. If the cards seem stacked against any sympathy for this character, this strategy serves the purpose of shifting the narrative centre from the heroic qualities of male mythic figures to the object on which their fate seems to depend.

Most importantly, as it invites us to trace the vision of Emmeline to its origin in the history of men's fantasies about woman's sexuality, the novel shows the consequences of such fantasies in the creation of a female character: Emmeline is given no choice except to fulfil her prophetic imperative. For like the vision of Athena, goddess of wisdom and war, springing from the head of her male creator, birth frees her to become dangerous unless she is made sexless and remains so. In contrast to Markie's fantasies, Emmeline's story reveals desires and fears that not only account for her threatening behaviour, but express Bowen's empathy for her deadly character. That Markie is the immediate and appropriate target of Emmeline's rage explains neither its source nor the passive, withdrawn aspect of her character. Moreover, from whatever perspective we view her character, the question remains: why must she kill herself as she enacts her rage against her betraying lover?

This question frames the complexities and contradictions that individualise Emmeline's character, making her other than a mythic monster and therefore inviting the reader to decode the narrative's indirect strategies, to desist his or her own defensive reading and to empathise with an otherwise distanced and uncanny character. The answers to these questions, moreover, are not easily accessible as they are presented in language that both disguises and expresses the source of Emmeline's intense need. Statements which on the surface seem hyperbolic or melodramatic conflate or literalise Emmeline's deepest sense of herself, as when she confesses to Cecilia: 'I can't imagine myself without you' (175). Although the relationship between sisters-in-law seems like a backdrop against which the more dramatic romance is played out, Emmeline's statement privileges her need for Cecilia. At one level the two women live together for convenience after the death of Henry Summers, Cecilia's husband and Emmeline's brother. But as the statement above suggests, Emmeline's need for her sister-in-law goes beyond convenience, even beyond companionship. A typically melodramatic statement when it occurs between lovers begs to be taken more literally in this context.

Established early in the novel, Emmeline's lack of independence not only inspires her passion for an apparently strong man, but explains her tie to Cecilia. Without family of her own, Emmeline feels closest to her sister-in-law. The house they share becomes more than a convenience as Emmeline invests it with the warmth and nurture she desires from Cecilia. Thus she tells Cecilia's fiancé, Julian Tower: 'This house is Cecilia' (192). This confluence of house and woman intensifies Emmeline's earlier statement about Cecilia, designating a need for sustenance on which Emmeline's sense of being, of survival, depends. Her sister-in-law's marriage plans are then tantamount to abandonment, destroying any hope that Emmeline will be sustained. Without Cecilia, Emmeline feels: ' "if I died . . . it wouldn't . . . be very noticeable" ' (192). Totally dependent on another for a sense of herself, on this level, Emmeline's character cannot even be differentiated. She is but a shadow of needs projected onto other objects and persons.

Emmeline's frustrated need for a nurturing and sustaining place is thus projected onto Markie, as confirmed by her reaction to the telegram announcing Cecilia's engagement. Using Markie's body to comfort her, she feels the loss of Cecilia:

. . . something slid down in her like a dead weight. Timber by timber, Oudenarde Road fell to bits . . . She saw the door open on emptiness: blanked walls as though after a fire. Houses shared with women are built on sand. She thought: 'My home, my home'. (208)

From this perspective, Emmeline craves from Markie not only adult sexuality, but a form of intimacy she seeks from Cecilia. It is the wish to be affixed to one who is perceived as capable of giving life and nurture to one 'still unborn'. At the height of their tryst in Paris such fusion is portrayed as Emmeline's heart's desire, but as with Edward Tilney, Markie's fear:

An intense sense of being each fused so close to the other as to be invisible, a fusion of both their senses in burning shadow obscured for the two . . . for Emmeline, Markie looking at her was in an instant of angry extinction as though he would drown. (141)

To enact a fantasy of dissolving the bonds between self and other may effect permanent union, but at the expense of someone's life. Such a fantasy explains Bowen's conflation of women and houses in all her work. It highlights the desire of an infant for the mother who is perceived as a nurturing holding place.

Couched in the structure of a domestic sub-plot, the fantasy of nurturing space becomes the gauge by which the novel tests the formation of female character. The images which designate fantasy reveal the ideological and psychological assumptions underlying the mythic splits of female character. Unlike Cecilia, who 'never seems to be happy when she is not in a train', Emmeline is energised only by fantasies of family homes which appear to her 'like some image of childhood, unaccountably dear but remote' (15,63). Although Emmeline also spends her life on the move, running her agency, travelling and socialising, she is 'distracted' and 'solitary', withdrawn, like Lady Elfrida, into herself, except when she is at home with Cecilia (21). Emmeline's frenetic movements between home and the outside world chart her futile attempts to find herself. But her expectations are betrayed by the coldness of those homes in which she seeks human feeling, such as Markie's 'theatre' or at Farraways, the country estate of her aunt and uncle. Compared to a dead Roman villa, this house, like all others in the novel, exists as a wish-fulfilment fantasy turned nightmare. They represent the impossibility of fulfilment in exactly those domestic arenas that appear to contain it.

Without a family home to lodge her needs, Emmeline is made to float in space which cannot provide self-definition. In this sense, her character is displaced and deformed, not just by mythologising it, but by a psychology for which Bowen shows there are no narrative remedies. By attributing fantasies of nurturing space to Emmeline, the novel locks her into a way of imagining herself that will be self-defeating. Such fantasies recall female characters who belong to a time and tradition which validate social and historic realities as contexts for self-discovery. If she were solely a character in a realistic novel she would ultimately be formed by domestic space, even if she were made to suffer there. As 'the step-child of her uneasy century', however, she is created in a time when fantasies of nurturing family homes are being questioned as a plot to form female character, a time when belief in a stable external reality and a knowable self is over (63). Endowing Emmeline with a psychology undercuts her mythic character, but her mythic qualities show her intrapsychic nature to be controlled by forces beyond her needs. Without an essential self, desperately seeking nurture without really being nurturing herself, Emmeline can reflect the desires of others, projected onto her translucent character. Hence she can incarnate Markie's fantasies, becoming a living myth, slated for destructiveness without contradicting her basic 'gentleness'.

Fantasies of nurturing homes which destabilise Emmeline's character ossify Cecilia's, whose apparent self-sufficiency is shown to be just another myth. As Emmeline thinks about Cecilia's inability to love since the death of Henry Summers, the narrator takes over to compare the loss of a loved one to 'a great house . . . destroyed by fire' which leaves a 'cold sky' akin to a cold heart (99). The sense conveyed by these images is that the loss of love and a stable self derive from the loss of a nurturing environment. In this novel every house appears as a fantasy of dispossession and loss, representing both the character of the child whose craving for nurture remains unfulfilled and the woman who does not nurture. Bowen uses Cecilia's abandonment of the wish for a nurturing family home to problematise the formation of female character in domestic space. Cecilia's withdrawal becomes the mirror image of Emmeline's infantile needs – the failure of the mother-figure to meet them. The escape from domestic ties suspends Cecilia between two displaced characterisations. Eminently pragmatic, Cecilia is the quintessential realistic character. But she is none the less, like Emmeline, 'mysterious' (246).

If the novel supplies Cecilia's motivation, it also presents her development as a compromise without resolution, 'at a standstill, her plot only half spun out' (991). Her 'frightened heart repair[ed] in small ways' defends itself in refusing to make a nurturing family home, not just for Emmeline, but for Julian and his orphaned niece (99). Refusing the role of nurturer, she resists incorporation into a mythic split and into a fantasy of fusion, but such a strategy 'dwarf[s]' Cecilia's character (99). As she seeks autonomy in the extreme, Cecilia is frozen, another version of Emmeline and the logical extension of another dominant perception of women. The failure of this alternative for female character is confirmed by Cecilia's self-limiting attempts at reality and myth testing. Avoiding the pitfalls of traditional female sexuality – nurturing or erotic – she becomes asexual. This perspective shows that if female characters cannot survive myths of their sexual power or of their need for attachment, avoidance does not create an alternative. It only transforms her into a mutant of the very character whose perception she represents: a male.

Cecilia is not unlike Markie. Where Markie's dread of Emmeline exposes his fear of intimacy, Cecilia's choice of the tepid Julian Tower (his surname glosses Markie's fantasies of Emmeline) reveals her own penchant for uninvolvement. Markie and Cecilia are both restless, rootless people, 'without sympathy, with just such a cold material knowingness' (7). And just as Cecilia is haunted by a fallen house, so Markie is disturbed by a tract of houses which remind him of 'great gabled carcases . . . bloated as thought by corruption' (56). The avoidance of domestic intimacy has sustained them both, but like the cold houses which repel Emmeline's quest for sustenance, Cecilia and Markie are rotting inside. They cannot be attracted to each other because Cecilia rejects fantasies of nurture and sexuality while Markie is shaped by both. The similarities between Markie and Cecilia undercut myths of female sexuality by undermining myths of male sexuality. The apparent strengths of male sexuality turn out to be based on the incorporation of a fantasy about women which is destructive to both sexes. Needing women to be both nurturing and erotic threatens the libertine who also fears the abundance of her gifts. Male fantasies of female nurturance and sexuality combine in Markie's fear of suffocation when Emmeline plies him with hampers of food during a weekend at a country cottage and in Paris in the vision of their sexual fusion which threatens to drown him.

Through Emmeline, *To the North* shows the inevitable consequences of basing female character on the myth of her sexual destructiveness. She enacts, with mythic justice, what men desire and fear, demonstrating how men contain the object of their fear and desire by making it an artifact to be worshipped and desired but now harmless.[12] Emmeline's metamorphosis results when intense need and loss are transformed into boundless rage. The images of her evolution are monstrous because they literalise the desires and power of infantile and adult sexuality. The needy infant becomes omnivorous, while the alluring woman is castrating. Worse, each side of her character is infused with the other until the rage felt by the deprived infant is enacted as acts of castration and murder while the sexually powerful woman enacts her infantile need to fuse with her love object. In terms of the narrative which demystifies Emmeline's character by psychologising it, sexual experience has satisfied her need to close the intolerable separateness she has endured. Markie's desertion is thus so debilitating, she totally loses her capacity to express herself in words. Looking 'all to bits', like her broken home and like Markie's fantasy of her, she reforms herself into the mechanism by which to integrate her desperate need for symbiotic wholeness (224).

In the last scene in the novel, Bowen consolidates her pattern of images to depict how a still powerless and voiceless woman fulfils her needs. Two contradictory states – stillness and speed – characterise Emmeline's quest for selfhood. Driving herself and Markie northward, she uses both her passivity and aggression to retreat from him, to become an entity to herself, untouchable and an instrument of her own volition. With 'speed, mounting through her nerves . . . [with] the startled wildness of flight', she races to a 'not-quite oblivion', beyond the reality of their struggle and certainly beyond fantasies of family homes, creating, paradoxically, 'a healing stillness' (242, 243). Character is generated here by the drama of unconscious and ambivalent desires for attachment and separation. Ignoring Markie's pleas uttered 'with the last calm of impotence', Emmeline crashes her car, fulfilling male and female fantasies (245). In this narrative, a woman's passion emerges from her state of withdrawal, unleashing the aggression necessary to decimate self and object in an instantaneous fusion. Total control thus serves a symbolic achievement of omnipotent oneness in the final resting place – death.

The interlocking narratives of Markie and Emmeline's romance and that of the formation of Emmeline's character trace her rage to helpless dependency. The only power Emmeline is given to mitigate her helplessness and to enact her rage is her sexuality. The need to fuse with the source of nurture accompanies the need to fuse with the source of all perceived power. The parallel structure of Emmeline's need for Cecilia and for Markie constitutes a transference of need for maternal power onto the male sexual love object. As a man, successful and important, perceived as empowered and in control, Markie is the appropriate target for the need to fuse with power in order to become powerful. By fusing with Markie sexually, Emmeline appropriates phallic power, producing in the novel the image of her as phallic woman. The novel ultimately reveals that for women, expressing and gaining power through sexuality is a precarious exercise at best. For as Bowen shows, women base their dubious desirability on an internalised and still prevailing myth that every innocent virgin has as her counterpart a deadly Circe. All of this takes place, however, as Emmeline's actions are interpreted by the narrator's imagery. Emmeline is given no consciousness by which to be held responsible. As a character, she is a somnambulist, sleepwalking through her mythic role. Nevertheless, this portrayal results in Markie's castration and death.

Such an interpretation would, of course, render a woman's sexuality and desire for power inherently destructive, not only to her lover on whom she depends to become whole, but to herself. For when used to satisfy a regressive need for fusion, sexuality not only denies wholeness and empowerment, but fulfils a fantasy of destroying the object on which it depends. Underlying the novel's interlocking narratives is this expression of women's paradoxical fear of endless and childlike dependency and of their insatiable sexual aggression. The novel's expression of the desire and fear of fusion and power has meaning for any consideration of the formation of female character. The toleration of fluid boundaries between self and other in any stage of development is impossible without the integration of eroticism, aggression and nurture historically denied female character.[13] Until that integration is imagined, separating these qualities will reproduce myths of women which remain threatening to their sense of being and which perpetuate and legitimate men's fears.

Analysing the formation of Emmeline's character still leaves the question of the author's relation to the fantasies propelling the characters. Despite the critique of myths about women in the narrative structure and the empathetic portrait of a deprived and powerless woman, Markie's fears are substantiated. Why would Bowen write a novel confirming myths about women's sexual aggression? The answers are bound up with the interlocking narratives which offer not just a rejoinder to myths about women, but a complex view of the nature and place of women's sexuality. Disguised by the melodramatic surfaces of Markie and Emmeline's romance and by opaque language, the mythic narrative and its rejoinder represent the position of a woman writer both comfortable in the traditions in which she works and critical of them. Through her narrative strategy, Bowen demystifies the character of women. Playing male and female fantasy against each other until they destroy each other, she leaves us with the character of Cecilia as a compromise position deriving from the need to 'live how one can – it is meaner living, gaudy, necissitous, full of immediate pleasures like the lives of the poor' (99). Curbed by social convention, even a sophisticated woman's sexuality is an unknown entity as it is not entirely free to express itself. Feelings of intense sexuality are therefore relegated to experiences which limit it through subterfuge or which are contained by literary conventions within which the imagination must work to find an audience. Testing the limits of female sexuality through her multifaceted female characters, Bowen imagines that without limitations they might very well be destructive. Through Emmeline and Cecilia, Bowen shows her own compromised frustration about the fate of women's sexuality as she imagines it. She reveals the frustrated desire of women to find sustenance and self-definition outside of domestic spaces and nurturing roles, to become empowered to control their destinies, but also to express the fear that given what they are taught to believe about themselves, power in their own hands may be a deadly illusion.

4 *The House in Paris*

In her fourth novel, *The House in Paris*, Elizabeth
Bowen develops a structure and style which dramatise
the symmetry and tension between a child yearning for his
mother and a woman who chooses not to mother.[1] Three
separate but interdependent parts of the novel mirror the
impact of maternal silence and domestic spaces on the
characters of a nine-year-old boy, Leopold, and his mother,
Karen Michaelis. Parts one and three portray Leopold's
alienated 'Present'; the middle discloses Karen's conflicted
'Past', explaining her absence from her son's present.[2] But
more, the past taunts the present; the presence of the past
in the minds of the characters reflects their desire for and
resistance to reconciliation. Because Bowen makes past and
present so dramatically palpable, the gaps between sections
are equally evocative. Suggesting emptiness, these places
which divide Leopold's story from that of his mother
are spatial and temporal metaphors. They represent the
mother's absence and silence, communicating to him that
his existence is denied, and therefore that his mother has
betrayed and dispossessed him. The tensions among three
separate but interdependent sections relating two stories
become equivalent to the conflicting desires and fears
which keep mother and child separated yet attached.[3]
The painfully ambivalent but incalculable bond between
children, mothers and houses that Bowen evoked in *The
Last September, Friends and Relations*, and *To the North* is
exposed here as an inexorable determinant of character.

Constructing the novel as a whole and as separate
stories, Bowen creates a narrative form which signifies
connection and detachment. Connection is conveyed by the
relationship between a story about a woman's ambivalence

about self-discovery, motherhood and home and one about a child's desperate need for maternal reunion. As we discover along with Leopold that his mother will not appear, each of their stories is given an independent voice and integrity – they are detached. The two stories, like the two characters, provide alternative perspectives to the novel's themes. Read together, they not only reconcile seemingly irreconcilable characters and stories, but suggest as well an imaginative space that replaces the damaging effects of domestic space. In this way Bowen's narrative form also critiques assumptions in the domestic novel about maternal responsibility and self-determination. The metaphoric interchange of mothers and houses represents a struggle for power, not only among fictive characters, but over the effects of different kinds of plotting on the formation of character.

Fantasies of betrayal and dispossession, self-determination and oppression are enacted in this novel by two narrative modes representing two renditions of domestic space. The gothic tale of Mme Fisher and her house in Paris and the realistic story of Mrs Michaelis and her Regents Park town house work in tandem and in opposition. This strategy acts out the conflicted relations between men and women and mothers and children, relationships in which sexual identity is both formed and destabilised. These conflicts and their resulting terrors connect gothic and realistic narratives, showing why, as Bowen said, 'we have everything to dread from the dispossessed' (*BC* 455).

The plot is shaped by Karen's absence from three crucial elements of the novel: she is missing from Leopold's first nine years, from the meeting she promises him, and from the first and last sections of the novel. Leopold's wish for his mother bridges her absence and the novel's three sections. Expressed initially as a fantasy in which he magically commands her presence, the wish is an antidote to his isolation and her absence. The fantasy appears first at the beginning of Karen's story in which he never appears, and then reappears in her reverie on the night she conceives him and expresses her ambivalence about motherhood. As it appears in her reverie, Leopold's wish for his mother therefore seems projected onto her fear of his presence. The child's needs, however, are ignored by the mother who paradoxically seemed to will his conception but deliberately chooses not to bring him home. A 'dread' of Leopold as being 'more than a little boy' – as being her 'enemy' – inspires Karen to keep him in her fantasies but not in her life (215, 155). Her actions counter Leopold's wish to make her his 'every desire', to create her 'in his image' (62). Because of her ambivalence, however, Karen is haunted by her son, a state of mind which both confirms and rejects his presence.

Bowen uses fantasy in this novel as an imaginative space where characters find refuge from their failed expectations of family homes. In turn, women's ambivalence about domestic space becomes a determinant of narrative form. Compelled by her relation to her mother and home, Karen is a mother *in absentia* for much of her story. She acts out conflicts which link all the houses, mothers and children in the novel. In turn, Karen's sheltered past informs and inheres in Leopold's transient present. Among Bowen's great achievements in this novel is showing how women's ambivalence about enforcing traditional family values affects the shape of the domestic novel.[4] Bowen's concern with the tradition of family homes is expressed in this novel as a psychological drama where houses embody a wish for continuity. The arena where parents and children struggle for individuation and attachment must itself remain stable for its combatants to survive. Karen's home, upper middle-class Chester Terrace, embodies the Michaelis's stability, providing considerable incentive for their child to remain faithful to her world; yet 'this was the world she sometimes wished to escape from' (71). This family home provides the basis for Bowen's exploration of the relationship between women's aggressive urges and family values. In order to be nurtured by a world which values constraint as life-sustaining, Bowen's heroine must turn against her own energy, that is, her urge to express her sense of an individual self. No sooner does she sleep with Max, the alien lover who threatens her family's values, than she yearns to return to her home.

Bowen's narrator notes how family values, represented by the domestic novel, diffuse women's aggression:

> [Karen] had been born and was making her marriage inside the class that in England changes least of all. The Michaelis lived like a family in a pre-war novel . . . Their relatives and old friends, as nice as they were themselves, were rooted in the same soil. Her parents saw little reason to renew their ideas, which had lately been ahead of their time and were still not out of date. . . . Nowadays, such people seldom appear in books; their way of life, though pleasant to share, makes tame reading. . . . up against no one, they are hard to be up against. Karen had had no reason to quarrel with anything, no dull times to be impatient in. . . . (70–71)

As in *The Last September*, as generations duplicate themselves, so individuality is lost. This later work charts the generative purpose of the rage concealed in women bred in 'the same soil'. Through her struggle for the right to be, Karen discovers that the reason 'they are so hard to be up against' lies in her mother's empty yet suffocating house; ironically, the security and rationality – the domestic realism of Chester Terrace – are disturbing, not soothing. Karen's mother is a discrete and discreet presence. In her home emotion is expressed only through prudent gestures – a hand reaching out tentatively, a silent tear falling. Retreating from the anarchic possibility of emotion, Mrs

Michaelis responds to Karen more like a 'statue' than a person (170). Decorum, the safety valve which 'keeps the lid on', is more than a style of behaviour; it is the substance of life at Chester Terrace.

Suppression of feeling protects mother and daughter from secret ambivalence; 'a wave of silence' expresses the wish and fear that one only begins and ends with identification with the other (168). Looking at each other 'closely but from a distance' creates a space in which child and mother play out their wish to be attached yet separate from each other. In this silent communication, they question and yet back away from finding out whether they can exist without either affirming or denying the presence of the other (170). When Mrs Michaelis discovers that Karen has spent a weekend with Max, she does something which creates an empty space that haunts Karen, foreshadowing the silent distance Karen later creates between herself and Leopold. Mrs Michaelis tears off a telephone message from the friend with whom Karen was supposed to be staying, leaving its imprint on the next page. By witholding knowledge but indicating that she has it, Karen's mother stages a painful *détente* between women as mother and as child. Karen senses that her mother 'would rather feel me almost hate her than speak', a strategy which defends the mother from the daughter's 'resistance' to their distance (174). The love that Karen craves precludes distance; it 'is obtuse and reckless; it interferes' (174). The force of the child's demands threatens to overwhelm the mother's sense of any self beyond motherhood. Protecting her home as a 'prison . . . museum' which preserves her power to set limits, the mother will ignore the child's transgression, as Karen realises: 'She has made me lie for a week. She will hold me inside the lie till she makes me lose the power I felt I had' (161).

Paradoxically, in a house where separation defines relationships, silence is not only an absence, but an assaulting presence, eradicating boundaries necessary to a sense of autonomy. A mother's 'mute eyes', like 'a searchlight that dipped into every valley', become a force enacted by the house itself (172,133)

> . . . the house with its fixed eye was compelling Karen. . . . Unconscious things – the doors, the curtains, guests Mrs. Michaelis – lent themselves to this savage battle for peace. Sun on the hall floor steps upstairs in the house had this same deadly intention to not know (173).

Like Lady Naylor's survival strategy in *The Last September*, denial only confirms that mothering does not make sense of the traditions which order the world of women. Silence becomes the last defence against such knowledge, particularly as it keeps children on a leash between dependence and rebellion. Both kinds of behaviour, however, only affirm the dubious power of mothering. As in Karen's denial of Leopold, a mother's silence insures the dispossession of both mother and child.

Karen ends her mother's silence by betraying the 'nice', 'tame' world of her parents, a holding environment which has sustained her too well. Her strategy, however, reflects her ambivalence toward such stability. She takes two lovers: Max Ebhart, Anglo-French and half Jewish, is like his son, an 'enemy' to her world and Ray, whom she says, 'was my mother', is its representative (154). Each man glosses the relationship between nurturing space and the ordering of sexual identity in the domestic novel. Max fulfils Karen's wish for passion, but not for independence or self-expression. His rootlessness encourages Karen's romantic fantasies about selfhood while demonstrating how impossible it is for a male character based on exotic lineage – difference – to fulfil either his selfhood or hers in a plot of domestic realism. Given her conflicted desires for a 'margin of uncertainty' and for security, Karen imaginatively transforms Max's difference into 'a touch of Ray . . . : domestic man' (69,108). In her efforts to create distance between what her mother stands for and some as yet amorphous idea of what she would like to be, Karen fuses the men's personae and confuses her sense of her own needs with theirs. Her actions show the effects of a narrative form built on the ideology of individual character but providing no self-determining outlets for a woman other than to submerge herself in the domestic needs of male character. Desiring the irreconcilable, Karen betrays the domestic codes assigned to women so that they will sustain the world which suffocates them: courtship, marriage, and family. She takes Naomi's fiancé for her lover while engaged to Ray; she bears a child who can have no legitimate claim to her world, and she betrays him by giving him away.

Through Karen's adventure of self-discovery, Bowen shows how combining sexual melodrama with the domestic novel is a trap for a character based on an ideology of individualism. For what emerges from Karen's 'revolution' is that being a lover turns out to be no escape from being a mother or a child (152). First, she cannot get through her one night with Max without thinking of Leopold as 'something that had to be' (153). Then, the consequences of the act designed to prove her an individual adult recast her as an undifferentiated character: dependent child. Retreating from being depended upon she returns to Chester Terrace to be mothered. But this only deals her individuality a double blow: she becomes the mirror image of her own dependent child, but she also replicates the witholding mother by disposing of her child. Like a child, Karen relies on 'word magic' to imagine away the consequences of her actions, but her effect is more lethal than she imagines. Karen's 'revolution' kills her mother, who plays her assigned role to the end, ensuring that the rebel's only option is to replay maternal control and vulnerability. Karen's actions portray the opposed yet interdependent scenarios of mother and child: the child's insatiable demands to be mothered and yet to be autonomous – indeed omnipotent – are both fulfilled and punished by having the mother die of doing her job too well. In response, the mother's desire to save herself from being absorbed and lost in the child's demands is fulfilled and punished by her death.

Compressing such an overdetermined relationship into the structure of a realistic narrative highlights the intense feeling beneath its play of manners and morals. Bowen's personification of Chester Terrace exposes the non-rational within the rational. In this novel she shows that the alignment of the realist tradition with traditional family values is purely defensive. The language of upper middle-class civility and restraint conceals how the domestic novel constrains the formation of female character. It expresses a woman's fulfilment only in terms of home management and mothering. In this novel the house is a metaphor mediating between the constraints placed on female character in the realist tradition and the subversion of those constraints in a gothic setting. In Bowen's portrait of the house in Paris, the consequences of such constraints are played out as a woman's rage dismantles family values.

In Paris, so far from the spirit and style of London, Mme Fisher protects her own 'bounds of propriety' with 'supernatural' omnipresence (102–103): 'Caring for nothing, she seemed to keep every happening . . . in her lit up mind. Her eyes still looked through the door . . . ' (56). Her claustrophobic house signifies not only lack of privilege and unrepressed passions, but the rage endemic to psychological imprisonment:

The inside of [the Fisher's] house . . . was antagonistic. . . . Nothing seemed to be natural; objects did not wait to be seen but came crowding . . . each with what amounted to its aggressive cry (24).

The fairy-tale quality of the house suggests a place where nightmares come to life, where fantasies of maternal control, sexual power and dispossession are enacted along with their imagined consequences. Contrasted with Mrs Michaelis's genteel but enervated tradition, Mme Fisher's mysterious powers represent a wish for imaginative outlets. Impoverished by the death of her husband, Mme Fisher portrays connections between economic and psychological constraints on women and the roles they are made to take in domestic and romantic novels. Turning her home into a finishing school, Mme Fisher is finished off by playing the part of a surrogate-mother who parodies all of the punitive limitations and gains none of the satisfactions of the original. Whatever social or literary tradition her house serves, it parodies, for Mme Fisher and her daughter Naomi are given no sense of purpose, no privilege, and indeed are imprisoned in their non-nurturing relationships to each other, to the young women on whom they wait, and in the house they support. The inversion of domestic space signified by the house in Paris, squeezed into its street, squeezing the life out of its keepers, produces an image of a sealed tomb. Bowen's evocation of the house compresses the conventions of domestic space. Although houses are usually interpreted as representing women's interior space and unconscious minds, the house in Paris also evokes both the imprisonment of a woman and her revenge. The house in Paris enacts Bowen's nightmare of dispossession.

Like the house in London, Mme Fisher's house embodies a struggle between mother and daughter for the meagre assets they inherit in a family home. Without external stimuli or affirmation to energise them, they turn against each other. Like Karen, Naomi acts out the limits of romantic love. She becomes engaged to Max, a poor bet, between his intrigues with her mother and with Karen. Self-enclosed and unsatisfied, the passions of Mme Fisher and her daughter reflect the destinies family homes

and romantic plots prescribe for women. Like a house of
mirrors which distorts everyone into grotesque parodies
of each other, this house of domestic fiction collapses
differences among female and male lovers and mothers
and children. This novel suggests that when conventions
of romantic love are wedded to family values, everyone
is reduced to the character of dependent child. Max's
entanglements with Karen, with Mme Fisher, and with
Naomi depict efforts to break into and out of the family
homes which entrap them all.

Through Max and Karen's love affair, Bowen dramatises
how domestic and romantic plots imprison male and female
character. The *ingénue*'s desire for her lover is no sign of
independence; it only replays her crush on him when she
lived at Mme Fisher's as an art student. Her creative
talent, however, paves the way only for the pursuit of
romantic love. Like her son, Karen expects to change
her life by inventing a fictional character. Her 'flamboyant
flowering' entraps Max, who responds to her as though
his life depends on it (108). Max's character is just right
for conversion into an artifact by women's imaginations.
His 'touchy sensitivity', his tendency 'to outlaw himself',
qualify him for a young girl's 'natural love of the cad' (117,
108). His character neatly fits Karen's desire for 'excess'
and 'suffer[ing]', her 'loving art better than life . . . and
need[ing] men to be actors' (107). The women in his life
cast Max as a stock figure in romance fiction. He is a cad
because he has been made one; he has no life of his own.[5]
He not only lacks the capacity to invent and carry out
a deceitful plot, his every move is predictable, whether
he fails Naomi's test of his character or fulfils Karen's
romantic whims. Seduced by the vision of 'an unattackable
safe place', the rootless Max sacrifices his autonomy to the
domination of women who must undo his character to test
the limits of theirs (162).[6]

Karen's seduction of Max reverses the realist tradition.

As her passion prevails and mirrors Mme Fisher's, the gothic takes over. The family home has been subverted, as decorum and social position have been traded for sexual intrigue and its equally strong passion, revenge. But Bowen manipulates the gothic tradition to show how passion, when used to wield power over others, paralyses female character even as it destroys the cad. Although their tryst in Boulogne is an 'escape', its 'utter silence' commands the lovers like the haunted houses in London and Paris (152,144). Max can barely wait to write to Naomi that he has betrayed her and, of course, her mother. Karen observes that her lover 'almost writes to be watched. . . . So we were not alone' (158). Max and Karen are not free agents. In the war for self-determination between mothers and children, Bowen portrays the literary and social history of a woman who uses motherhood for power she cannot find anywhere else. Her repressed energy emerges as revenge, a form of expression which in this novel undercuts the differences between realist and gothic plots to show how literary differences between gender mirror the social. Vindicating her own frustrated self-determination, Mme Fisher prevents Max from achieving independent manhood; indeed, his dependence on her is greater than his desire to escape with Karen, as he tells his young lover:[7]

> Till this year, I have not tried to separate what she made me from what I am. From the first, she acted on me like acid on a plate. . . . as she saw me, I became. (138)

As in all of Bowen's work, women are 'corrosive' – they function like acid, corroding the characters of others and themselves (138). This occurs when women convert their thwarted need for self-expression into the power to replicate themselves in another. This displacement expresses women's rage at assuming responsibilities they cannot afford when they are left to uphold the traditional order abrogated by weak or absent men. Without access to the economic, social or rhetorical powers which represent that order, they project their need onto the other. Thus Mme Fisher would reshape Max's character by etching into it the aggression she cannot otherwise enact. But the heir to such a legacy inherits a double dose of weakness. Children inherit the lack of an effective language. Dying too early to give his son the power of a native tongue, Max's father leaves only silence. Debilitating to the son, 'electric silence' is eagerly taken up by Mme Fisher as revenge against the silent dependence of women (133). Karen's problem is the reverse of Max's, but the mirror of Mme Fisher's, and the revelation of her mother's. She finds that the only language she knows is a trap. Her people use language as a 'cushion' against difference and change, against the invasion of such rage as Mme Fisher's.[8] This kind of silence, however, while too diffuse to be converted into aggression – a weapon – is seized by Karen as a defence which paralyses her. For as it mocks the strategy of her mother and Mme Fisher, silence shows the deadliness of either sexual passion or maternal control as a tool for empowerment. Her secret affair, like her childbearing, only replicates all silence in this novel which assaults and corrodes character.

The silence between Max and Mme Fisher conceals yet exposes the 'evil' shaping the house in Paris and the entropy causing the collapse of the London house. When Max returns to Mme Fisher, his destruction is assured. Naomi's account of Max's suicide emphasises the inextricable and deadly bond between her mother and Max:

> I saw then that Max did not belong to himself. He could do nothing that she had not expected; my mother was at the root of him. I saw that what she had learnt about you [Karen] and him pleased her, that she had pleasure in it in some terrible way. . . . I saw then that

evil dominated our house . . . I saw then that all her life her power had never properly used itself, and that now it had used itself she was like the dead, like someone killed in a victory. . . . She said: 'He cut his wrist across, through the artery, to hurt me . . . He struck my self, himself, my knowledge of him . . . He needed so much to escape'. (182–183)

While Mme Fisher's character exposes what threatens Mrs Michaelis and Karen in their roles as mothers, Max's character reveals what threatens Karen, Naomi, and Leopold in their roles as children. Mme Fisher enacts what is so terrifying about mothers in the child's worst fears. She nurtures Max so that he will pursue what she desires but cannot have herself – the privilege and power synonymous with patriarchy. Max, however, without a language and tradition of his own, is a poor imitation of his mentor. Stumbling on her methods, he falls into her trap. Using his aggression to become a lover instead of a partner, he betrays the woman who has no power without projecting her aggression onto him. Mme Fisher taunts Max to free himself, but imprisons him in a relationship which reflects only her needs, a relationship Bowen aptly calls 'a death cell' (182). Unable to transcend the limits defining her gender or his, Mme Fisher unmans Max in an attempt to reshape her womanhood.

The imagery describing this desire suggests the realm of fantasy, not social reality. For although social and economic factors shape these characters, the images expressing their feelings convey non-rational, unsocialised need. Max experiences Mme Fisher as threatening to engulf him with omniscient powers, to take over his character – his maleness. The only freedom and retaliation the enslaved and enfeebled man can imagine finally, is suicide. Yet Max's suicide is the logical consequence of the novel's critique of external determinants – the literary and social forms which subvert the interdependence of mother and child and their empowerment. His death points to the destructiveness of social codes which attribute overwhelming power to the role of mothering while undermining the power of women to be self-determining. Portraying Mme Fisher as the witch-mother shows how splitting women into images of good and bad – of nurturance and aggression – creates female character as threatening. Through Mme Fisher, Bowen shows female character stuck in her chrysalis, a step past Lois Farquar's cocoon, a more self-conscious and critically alert Emmeline, but without access to metamorphosis. Confined to bed by paralysis, her 'iron will' has quit at the stage of becoming a parody of sexual and creative energy – another gothic tale of failed self-creation – a female combination of Dr Frankenstein and his monster: 'webbed down, frustrated, or, still more, like someone cast, still alive, as an effigy for their own tomb' (48). With no other form of expression after Max dies, the widow's aggression turns inward: 'she burn[s] herself out for nothing' (188).

The contrast between Mme Fisher's will and paralysed body indicates the terrible cost to a woman of using sexual passion and maternal domination for self-discovery and revenge against the limits imposed on it. To push motherhood or sexual energy to their extreme limit or to react against them, using them none the less, results in paralysis. At one level it is as though the female is petrified into a form mirroring male desire and fear of her sexuality. At another, her body reifies both her only outlet for expression and her revenge. Yet the narrative design shows that the energies trapped in Mme Fisher's body and home are necessary to life. Despite her brief and enigmatic appearances, Mme Fisher becomes the centre of the novel, presiding over the lives of the characters like a novelist – more particularly, a woman novelist, imagining extreme outlets because the realist tradition and realistic worlds offer none.[9]

Karen's voyage between the houses in Paris and London bridges the social and literary history as well as the psychology which shapes Bowen's female character. Because it is destructive, passion without the containment of motherhood is inadmissible at Chester Terrace. In Paris, because it is suppressed, passion is destructive, and yet its absence represents a wish for vitality. Karen's trip to a third house, an Irish house, connects Paris and London to the dangers Bowen locates in the traditional order of all family homes. Escaping her own 'aimless' life' at Mt Iris, her aunt and uncle's 'strange' house, Karen finds that it is 'silent' and 'inanimate', causing 'the you inside you [to] gather up defensively' (69,76–77).

These new unsmiling lights, reflections and objects are to become your memories, riveted to you closer than friends or lovers, going with you, even into the grave: worse they may become dear and fasten like so many leeches on your heart. By having come, you already begin to store up the pains of going away. From what you see, there is to be no escape. Untrodden rocky canyons or virgin forests cannot be more entrapping than the inside of a house, which shows you what life is. To come in is as alarming as to be born conscious would be, knowing you are to feel; to look round is like being, still conscious, dead: you see a world without yourself. . . . (77)

Recorded in silence, spoken to no one, Karen's thoughts reflect the activity of a woman engaged in a creative process that comes to a dead end. The imagery in the above passage derives from the impact of external reality on Karen's personal sensation. But the associations which give the imagery meaning remain within her consciousness, communicated second-hand through the narrator and mediated by a complex of other characters' needs and by narrative design. Such an indirect process of self-expression suggests that the lack of creative outlets produces a fantasy of terror. It depicts an aborted birth experience where the female self is absorbed by the ancestral home on which it depends, experiencing a living death. Such an experience, recalling Bowen's rendering of Anglo-Irish houses, shows that the order and tradition represented by family homes are nevertheless fatal to body and creative spirit.

If Karen's escape from houses turns out to be no escape at all, it is because Bowen shows the dubious security of relying on the order and tradition of domestic novels for the creation of female character. Karen's rebellion against domesticity and domination, however, only perpetuates them. As she avoids her mother, so she gives up her son, only to control his fate in her absence. Functioning as both powerful mother and powerless child, threatening to Leopold as she fears mother-figures herself, she is caught, like so many heroines in the history of the English novel, short of development.[10] She is assigned the role of arbiter of the moral and psychological development of others, but without self-determination. Her resulting frustration produces the very behaviour which justifies others treating her like a child. Her act of passion and conception of Leopold were events she willed, but which she comes to fear, and which paralyse her like the impotent witch-mother in Paris. When the narrative shifts from Karen's dilemmas of the past to Leopold's plight in the present, it highlights absence and silence: it does not portray the time between Leopold's birth and his ninth year or Karen's feelings about her child. As a result, Bowen shows her heroine condemned in two ways: significant action is over for Karen and her feelings about the son she desired yet abandoned, about her dead lover, about her husband, and about life outside domestic space, remain inchoate, representing a kind of silence which incapacitates her. When we next hear of her, she lies on a bed shuddering, refusing to speak, driving her 'knuckles into the pillow', in a hotel across a river from Leopold (215).

Ten years after her fateful act, this hysteria is the only way Karen can deal with the questions her husband and son ask her. Like Mme Fisher, the younger woman is frozen, unable to articulate her anguish or to act. The impulse to fulfil herself through the creation and rejection of male character – Max and his son – has led to another no-win situation, replicating Max and Mme Fisher. Karen's wish for Leopold turns out to be a double bind. It is the antidote to fears of aborted life and silence, but it also turns out to be a self-fulfilling prophesy of her fate in the hands of the domestic novel. Like 'the mark our hands did not leave on the grass', the power Leopold represents cannot be wished away (153):

> I cannot see him to see what a child would be like. Though there will not be a child, that is why I want to see him. If a child were going to be born, there would still be something that had to be. To-night would be more then than hours and that lamp. It would have been the hour of my death. I should have to do what I dread, see them know. There would still be something to dread. I should see the hour in the child. I should not have rushed on to nothing. (153)

Having a child, she realises, is 'poison', as it acts as 'some foreign thing' within her (154). Such fear represents the mother who is destroyed by having to be all-powerful and all-knowing while the child makes insatiable demands to be both part of and free of her. No matter how hard Karen tries to escape her child, she cannot. The double narrative produces a complex portrait of a woman whose quest for selfhood must include being a mother, whether she chooses to accept that role or not. Karen's motherhood even takes priority over her marriage; the idea of Leopold shapes the way Ray and Karen talk and fail to talk to each other, in fact, the way they make love (220). Her obsession with Leopold is even the cause, as she tells Ray, of her failure to bear their child.

If the fantasy controlling Karen's story recreates entrapment, the fantasy shaping Leopold's story suggests an antidote. Leopold imagines and indeed manages to get a mother who is never allowed to forget that he is the most important person in her life. Having asked the critical questions when he finds himself rejected for a second time – 'Why am I? What made me be?' – the child will receive no direct answer (67). But the placement of these questions in proximity to his mother's story suggests an indirect response to his dramatic query. She would, as he imagines her, speak 'without deception . . . She would have told what she had done without looking for motives' (68).

Actually, the meeting he had projected could take place only in heaven – call it heaven; on the plane of potential, not merely likely behaviour. Or call it art, with truth and imagination informing every word. Only there – in heaven or art, in that nowhere, on that plane – could Karen have told Leopold what had really been. (67)

Leopold's disappointment and artful imaginings are split between the end of the first section and the beginning of the last: positioned like two bookends propping up his mother's story. Surrounding the mother's story is the child's wish for the mother's recognition, for the right to be. In this way Karen's story is positioned as a kind of provisional compensation for her son's initial disappointment. For as the narrator tells us upon introducing Karen's story, 'this is, in effect, what she would have had to say' (68). It is as though the mother's story is created in response to Leopold's need to imagine his own version of her. Her story becomes a bridge between the domestic tale of mothering Karen chooses not to take part in and her own experience of suffocating, silent mothering. Hence Karen's character as mother and as child and the child's critical response to her choosing not to mother interact.

With no visible or audible sign and no memory to recapture the mother's presence, with no sense of her life or death, Leopold is suspended between fantasy and experience. The narrative structure suggests a process by which the abandoned and dispossessed child comes to grips with an inaccessible mother by having Leopold create her as an imaginative recapitulation of a reassuring past. In his fantasy Karen would speak the truth about them in a way that privileges his importance to her. He even invents a letter in which she writes to Naomi that 'Leopold is the only person I want' (45). Such a construction, however, denies the mother any reality separate from the child's wishes. A displaced person, Leopold will assert his own magic and displace reality. He will create the fiction that makes him real by supplanting his mother's absence with a story about her. Bowen suggests that until the child confronts the reality of his mother's absence, of her desire for autonomy, he invents her character as a solution to now knowing his past or his destiny. He becomes a storyteller.

Leopold's passage through the house in Paris calls attention to its fictionality: its gothic excesses provide an appropriate setting for children wishing 'to discover the power to crack the tomb and grow up to any height' (203). Stunted by his mother's absence, Leopold now imagines his ability to control her fate, and therefore his own. The narrator comments ironically on Leopold's transformation of his mother's absence into presence:

> Meetings that do not come off keep a character of their own. They stay as they were projected. So the mother who did not come to meet Leopold that afternoon remained his creature, able to speak the truth. (67)

His creature, however, challenges the child; like a budding Dr Frankenstein, providing another perspective to Mme Fisher's desires for self-expression, Leopold must face the creature's own story, and as it asserts its own reality, it turns out to be no comforting fantasy of mutual understanding. His mother has her own needs, her own 'will, act and thought':

> Her refusal became *her*, became her coming in suddenly, breaking down, by this one act of being herself only, his imagination in which he had bound her up. So she lived, outside himself; she was truly alive, truly. She set up that opposition that is love. (193,194)

Leopold's outburst in response to his mother's independence is presented with both empathy and critical distance. Henrietta, the slightly older and more cynical child who waits in transit with him, confirms Leopold's grief while witholding any comfort:

> At first each sob was like some terrible accident, then they began to come faster. He wept like someone alone against his will, someone shut up alone for a punishment: you only weep like that when only a room hears. . . . His undeniable tears were more than his own, they seemed to be all the tears that ever had been denied, that dryness of body, age, ungreatness or anger ever had made impossible – for the man standing beside his own crashed 'plane, the woman tearing up somebody's fatal letter, and dropping pieces drily into the grate, people watching their family house burn, the general giving his sword up – arrears of tears starting up at one moment's unobscured view of grief. (196)

The narrator takes over from Henrietta's thoughts to stress that Leopold's tears affirm 'the end of imagination' and coincide with the abandonment and dispossession necessary to leave childhood dependence behind (197).[11] Leaning on the same mantle where his father took his life, rejected by the same woman in the same way, Leopold will demonstrate an alternative model for the development of male character. His state of limbo – in transit – only marks the time when Leopold's questions are not addressed to thin air as they seem to be, but to the mother who could not hear except as he imagined she must.[12] In this novel about the potent effects of the imperative to mother on the formation of male and female character, Bowen constructs the fiction to keep mother and child apart yet interdependent, so as to assure the integrity of each.

The past and present sections of the novel simulate a 'dialogue' between mother and son while confirming that it never takes place. Although it breaks the silences shaping the novel, the dialogue also occurs as a silence, within their unspoken thoughts. As the separate but interpenetrating structure implies, the novel provides boundaries to each story and to the characters of mother and son while suggesting their interdependence. In this way the narrative structure is analogous to Bowen's attitude toward mother-child relationships as she dramatises them. She recognises not only their need for interdependence, but their fears of suffocation and violation. The structure limits the impulse to control for self-empowerment and its resulting incorporation of one object by another.

Bowen endorses both independence and limits by creating a character whose sense of reality requires the recognition of individual differences as well as mutual responsibility. The decisive action of Ray Forrestier not only affirms his own life, but suggests resolutions to the lives of the protagonists and to the structure of the work. Ray is a realist. Not given to wish-fulfilment fantasies about self-discovery, but constantly probing Karen's feelings, he is also capable of accommodating the reality of Karen's situation. For this reason he does not romanticise Leopold's pitiable situation. Instead, he assesses his relation to the boy with a jaundiced eye: 'This little brittle Jewish boy with the thin neck . . . was the enemy: she was right' (215). Taking Leopold away with him is Ray's attempt to mediate the threat of difference – to transform the child from a dreaded alien/enemy to an ordinary person – to likeness: 'If he were here with us, he'd be simply a child, either in or out of the room. While he is a dread of ours, he is everywhere' (217).

While Ray's action breaks the deadly silences, Bowen problematises it. On the one hand, Ray acts empathically, activating Leopold's wishes: 'Egotism and panic, knowing mistrust of what was to be, died in Ray as he waited beside Leopold for their taxi to come: the child commanded tonight. I have acted on his scale' (239). Ray's ability to act for himself and Leopold appears to be cause for celebration: it mitigates the horrors which turn women into witches. His actions, however, call attention to the way realist plots allow male characters to be self-determining, but also the determiners of the fate of others. His sensitivity to Karen's plight and to Leopold's means that he does not have to accept their stories as gothic melodrama, as being determined by 'the dead silence behind Mme Fisher's door' (226). As he walks out on Karen's histrionics, the paralysing conflicts of mother-child relations seem to be translated into a more liberating resolution: the perceived rationality of paternal power. For Ray's lot is realistic and rational. His acceptance of Leopold, and admission that he has no definite, pre-arranged plans, his deployment of Mme Fisher as counting 'much less than you think', point to an ally of contingency who facilitates the open end of the novel (221). Yet Ray, we are told, insists a little too strongly on his staying 'free', especially as he feels 'the world had come to an end' as soon as he steps inside Mme Fisher's door (211).

The double narrative counterposes two plots and an overarching critique. In Ray's plot, conflicts are perceived and resolved pragmatically, as fitting into experience that is understood in external, social terms. The women's plot exposes Ray's as being formed by the same non-rational wishes and fears which underlie social experience and underwrite gothic tales. What Karen had to fear was that being dispossessed and fatherless, her son's only access to a birthright was to haunt her. Bowen shows that Leopold was born of a father who had to self-destruct in order for female character to overcome the contortions of romantic melodrama. Leopold has only one hope for his own character to survive: to be nurtured by plotting a different kind of environment. Between the gaps of this novel's three sections arises an alternative space and plot: a family home where rational social experience, as it has been shaped by patriarchal needs, is revised. Such a revision would recognise that what has been labelled non-rational is the judgement levied at female need. An alternative space would admit outlets for female self-expression as necessary for human growth. Paternal plotting, Bowen argues by implication, is what gives rise to the contortions of two major trends in the English novel. In the gothic plot a woman becomes either monstrous or weak and dependent because she fuses aggression, sexuality and motherhood, but has no desire to nurture and no environment to nurture her. In the realist plot a woman submerges her aggression in the care of her husband, home and children, causing her to betray her own womanhood.[13] Neither gothic nor realist plot recognises her individuality as a healthy difference.

The dilemmas of Bowen's female characters are mirrored in her own life and illuminate so much of the ambivalence she felt about the place of women's power in their homes. *The House in Paris* was written in 1934, four years after Bowen's father died. As the last of the Bowens, she inherited her ancestral home, a dubious honour which conflicted in part with Bowen's personal and professional ambitions. Having escaped her family's troubled past by making her life and career in England, she wanted and was obliged to return to Bowen's Court. But she was barely able to keep up the house, while she completely gave up on family tradition. Although she provided no heir and returned to Bowen's Court only in the summer, the idea of family homes haunted her creative imagination as dispossession haunts her characters. The Regent's Park town house on which Chester Terrace is based becomes the primary setting for Bowen's continuing exploration of the relationship between female character and the imperative to create a family home. In the coming years, as World War II makes the ideal of an ancestral home with an inherited sense of order and tradition an anomaly, Bowen examines the character of women who must turn inward to their own creative sensibilities to redesign domestic space and revise family values.

5 *The Death of the Heart*

The Death of the Heart, published four years after *The House in Paris*, is considered by many to be Bowen's crowning achievement.[1] Acclaimed for its contemporary treatment of the theme of innocence and disenchantment, Bowen's sixth novel traces the egocentric needs of child and adult as they are transformed into a recognition of mutual interdependence. *The Death of the Heart* is different from the earlier novels. Dispensing with gothic, mythic, and romance motifs, with mysterious, unexplained events, Bowen creates a realistic domestic novel of manners, using conventions of verisimilitude, multi-dimensional character, and forays into the characters' pasts through their own fully conscious recollections. An ensemble of characters forms the intertwined quests of a young girl for love, a family home and a sense of herself and of a married woman who resists such goals. Bowen portrays everyone in this work as capable of giving verbal expression to an understanding of those forces which paralyse characters in earlier works. This novel is composed of a process by which one woman on the brink of self-discovery and another who has lost her sense of herself free themselves from a haunting past by becoming interdependent. As Anna Quayne reads about herself in the diary of her sixteen-year-old ward, Portia, the two women negotiate the ground between daughterhood and motherhood. In doing so, they change the course of the domestic novel. In Bowen's hands, it is now about female character shaping herself in her acts of writing and interpretation.

More than any of the novels which precede it, *The Death of the Heart* suggests the possibility of change through the recognition that difference is integral to likeness. Enacted between two women set in opposition to each other, this recognition becomes a decisive move leading to an attempt at reconciliation between mother and daughter figures. For the first time in Bowen's fiction, female characters seize their own volition to make themselves the determining figures in a domestic novel. At the end, as they are about to meet each other at least half-way, the domestic novel has been wrested away from an enfeebled patriarchy and reinvigorated by women's interdependent stories.

Structuring the novel so that female characters are agents of their own doing and undoing leads Bowen to treat houses differently as well. Bearing no relation to a determining past, houses here do not embody family or cultural histories which provide clues to the meaning of characters' lives. Interestingly, there are no country estates in this novel to become elaborate symbolic structures. Instead, houses are the sum of the characters' discomforts in the present. In this way, the carefully ordered London town house, Windsor Terrace, and the chaotic seaside villa, Waikiki, reveal how homes and characters create each other. Bowen's realistic method also shifts her study of character. Portia's quest through the houses in which she finds neither answers nor love, shows that self-determination, the key to effecting change, must include full recognition and understanding of the past as well as responsibility for whatever one is in the process of becoming. In previous Bowen novels, the past paralysed women who found no way to deal with its patriarchal codes. In this work, the past is kept alive by a woman who fully understands its price – the aptly placed Quayne's housekeeper, Matchett. In addition to her relentless care of the furniture, Matchett takes care to remind Portia of the past Windsor Terrace is designed to ignore. Offering queries to the child as Mme Fisher did for Leopold, Matchett is unique in her success. For Portia is then given to question her life in the form that was liberating for her creator. She uses writing as a form of self-reflection and expression. As she sees the emptiness of the Quayne's 'air-tight rooms', as well as the confusions in other people's messy ones, she interprets these experiences in her diary (26–27).

Like other Bowen youth, Portia lives in a state of transit, but she alone is given the means to reconcile the past, her homelessness and a disturbing present. Like Leopold, Portia needs to know 'Why am I . . . What made me be?' At sixteen and not nine, however, she can activate her search for love and a life of her own. Having been dispossessed by the death of her parents, she awaits uncertain entry into a new home and family. Portia is the orphaned child of Irene and Mr Quayne, who married only after the first Mrs Quayne banished her straying husband once he confessed that the young widow he had been visiting in London was pregnant with his child. Mr Quayne's son by his first marriage, Thomas, and his wife Anna, not only inherit the child of this embarrassing 'aberration . . . the child of an old chap's pitiful sexuality', but find themselves threatened by the omnipresent demand of a parentless child for a family (246).

Unlike the rootless Leopold, Portia was raised lovingly by her mother before losing her. The brief but secure place in her mother's arms gave her the promise of unconditional love, but once orphaned, her expectations for nurture are betrayed. There are now no guarantees that she will be loved or develop a clear sense of herself in relation to a world she can understand. The novel is given its momentum by Portia's attempts to discover why the world cannot accommodate her needs. Although she grows up knowing the facts of her life story, Portia can only learn what they mean as she discovers the integrity of another woman's life and needs. In order for Portia to become a woman herself, her dead all-loving mother must be replaced by a resisting mother who is still struggling to learn what it means to be a woman.

Portia's quest consists of a rediscovery of her past,

its relation to the places signifying its disorder, and the feelings of those who would prefer it never happened. Portia's life with her mother illustrates how the myth of a woman finding self-definition through romantic love is actually self-denying, especially if she does not recognise its relation to domestic codes. Irene's hold on Mr Quayne's illicit love makes her unfit for the one environment which can accommodate her dependence and maternity – the traditional family home. Dependent on each other's sustaining love after Mr Quayne's death, Portia and Irene are forced to live in no particular place, without domestic responsibilities or social constraints, but without economic or social support as well. The self-protective way they see their transience as a game, however, foreshadows the relationship's tragic end and leaves Portia 'untaught', with no antidote to 'knowing that nine out of ten things you do direct from the heart are the wrong things' (56). As Portia's observation illustrates, without some kind of domestic tradition within which to struggle for self-determination, female character seems to have no foundation on which to become palpable and stable:

> If you always live in hotels . . . you get used to people always coming and going. They look as though they'd be always there, and then the next moment you've no idea where they've gone, and they've gone for ever. (48)

As Portia moves from one place to another, a compassionate narrator connects the disorders of her odyssey with her mother to the lonely order of Anna's stability:

> Only in a house where one has learnt to be lonely does one have this solicitude for *things*. One's relation to them, the daily seeing or touching, begins to become love, and to lay one open to pain. Looking back at a repetition of empty days, one sees that monuments have sprung up.

Habit is not mere subjugation, it is a tender tie: when one remembers habit it seems to have been happiness. So, she and Irene had almost always felt sad when they looked round a hotel room before going away from it for always. They could not but feel that they had betrayed something. In unfamiliar places, they unconsciously looked for familiarity. It is not our exalted feelings, it is our sentiments that build the necessary home. The need to attach themselves makes wandering people strike roots in a day: wherever we unconsciously feel, we live. (139–140)

The narrator's elegiac tone actually betrays an ironic attitude toward domestic space. The juxtaposition of habit, love and pain suggests that for Irene and Portia, the reliance on domestic order undercuts their ability to rely on their own feeling for a 'necessary home'. The passage thus undermines any sentimental notion of the promises we attach to homes and yet questions whether we can do without the idea of one.[2]

The narrator's attitude parallels Bowen's history and feelings about travelling with her mother when her father became ill. Despite her memories of an intense closeness, Bowen questions whether this experience of maternal love without domestic responsibility is idyllic, painful, illusory, or all three. For Portia's memory of 'giggling into eiderdowns . . . overcoming, as far as might be, the separation of birth', is tempered by other rhetorics (56). The narrator's glimpses into the homes of Portia's childhood – 'an out-of-season nowhere', the 'sunless hotel rooms, those chilly flats' – provides a gloss on Portia's memory (56,40). But the real shape of domestic life cannot become apparent to Portia until she loses her mother. Her subsequent entry into 'The World' signifies the illusory happiness invested in familiarity that prevents women from growing up to create their own world.

Anna's house, more than any in Bowen's work, illustrates how 'monuments' to domestic stability are built on conventions of the domestic novel. Details of class, such as address and style, reveal how an upper middle class creates a haven from the intrusion of chaotic realities. If domestic space is designed to protect women who in turn safeguard the family structure, the novel's critique suggests how the political implications of this defensive mechanism resonate in a wider realm. Bowen's concern with the dubious notion of a safe haven is particularly timely as her adopted nation began to feel threatened by signs of world disorder in 1938. Like the displacement of the Jew, Max Ebhart, in her earlier work, *The House in Paris*, *The Death of the Heart* resonates with emotional insecurities, exacerbated by political, social and economic conditions.

Anna, an interior decorator, has designed 2 Windsor Terrace to reflect a lack of personal concern. She and her husband, who are rarely found in the same room, are detached from each other and from identification with the past or with the difficulties of anyone else. Nowhere is this more apparent than in Thomas' below-level study, where he buries his passions in sleepy idleness while Anna entertains above. Unlike the 'sentiments that build the necessary home', the social and moral conventions which brace these stucco walls disguise and control discomforting feeling and realities. Gracious gestures, affecting poses and meticulously decorated rooms substitute for warmth and intimacy. But as Anna fills her cigarette case or lounges gracefully on a silk sofa, she also seems to parody the structure she gives her life.[3] Anna's house and submerged feeling recall Mrs Michaelis and Chester Terrace, but with an even more critical tone. Despite her efforts to design a home without feeling, Anna fails. For once Portia arrives, neither the Quayne's arch but weary repartee nor their studied detachment protect them from being exposed as betrayed and damaged. Everything about their house seems designed to reject nurture and support; its rooms betray some 'lack of life . . . some organic failure in its propriety. . . . there was no place where shadows lodged, no point where feeling could thicken' (42).

Anna has enclosed herself and Thomas in a domestic space that secludes them from the 'widened susceptibility' of love because 'it is felt at the price of feeling all human dangers and pains. . . . The attempt at Windsor Terrace to combat this may have been what made that house so queasy and cold. . . . In fact something edited life in the Quayne's house' (170,171). Like Portia, Anna is motherless, but has also betrayed her own desires by rejecting Robert Pidgeon, her first love. She married Thomas on the rebound because he demanded neither passion nor intimacy from her and seemed, like her, to take refuge in the style of their upper middle-class home.[4]

As in Bowen's earlier work, a woman's silence expresses her reaction to the constraints of the culture she inherits and marries. But in this novel, silence has no mysterious power; it dramatises a logical response to an unnatural breach: between a woman and the roles she has been given to believe constitute her essence – wife, lover and mother – keeper of the hearth. Anna's silence poses a crucial question for the domestic novel as purveyor of the ideology of the middle-class family. How can a woman writer use the language of the domestic novel which defines and limits her female characters? As she develops the relationship between Anna and Portia, Bowen recognises the language of this dominant form to be the basis for literary revision. Portia's presence violates the boundaries and silences protecting domestic space in its various significations. As an adolescent woman, she represents rebellion against the forms of authority which define her needs for her. But she rebels as well against complacency which is only a weary response to the moral and emotional confusions of traditional authority. Authority and responses to it are represented by the houses and rooms which shape Portia's quest.

Every house and room in this novel illustrates how Portia's quest for moral and emotional certainty is invariably threatening to domestic order. When the Quaynes go abroad for vacation, Portia is sent to Waikiki, the seaside home of Mrs Heccomb, Anna's childhood governess. Here, in the section labelled 'The Flesh', feeling appears more acceptable than at Windsor Terrace, but in fact is disguised and parodied by a less polished but even more conventional style of manners and morals. As personified by Mrs Heccomb, the house seems open and warm: 'you knew where everyone was, what everyone did – except when the noise they made was drowned by a loud wind' (135). What for the reader could be a pun on life's more obtrusive noises in this 'primitive state', does not strike Portia as disturbing at first (171). For Waikiki's 'many sensory hints . . . made [it] the fount of spontaneous living. Life here seemed to be at its highest voltage . . . a dynamo of free living' (171). Portia prefers Waikiki to Windsor Terrace because she thinks its 'unedited life' is self-revealing. Moreover, Waikiki reminds her of her life with her mother:

> You see, it's more like what I was accustomed to. At Anna's, I never know what is going to happen next – and here, though I may not know, I do not mind so much. In a way, at Anna's nothing does happen – though of course I might not know if it did. But here I do see how everyone feels. (192)

Portia realises only from experience that Waikiki's tumult, its 'behaviour that was pushing and frank', express confused feelings rather than openness (171). Daphne and Dickie Heccomb, also orphans, constantly break through the veneer of their 'naive propriety' to reveal a ruthless defensiveness embedded in constantly shifting standards of decorum. At Waikiki 'propriety is no serious check to nature – in fact, nature banks itself up behind it' (171). The way the house is always in danger of being damaged by the wind and the sea outside reflects the assaulting feelings of its inhabitants. Portia has yet to discover the hidden content in adult behaviour which connects the moral framework of her parents'confused lives to that of Thomas and Anna's fastidious order.

Although Waikiki's carelessness seems opposed to Windsor Terrace, it disguises a kind of 'necessary pattern' which ironically recalls Anna's hospitality (149). The easy, indifferent response of Daphne and Dickie to Portia's intrusive presence is the flip side of the Quaynes'. Instead of a refuge, both houses make 'refugees' of those like Eddie, who seek warmth, at their 'painted fires' (149). The defensive styles of both houses reveal how domestic arrangements of power distort character. Not surprisingly, Eddie's style both fits in and threatens the two houses. A marginal figure at Windsor Terrace, where Anna cautiously modulates their flirtation, Eddie is made 'a crook but . . . not a fake' by the sexual and moral codes of domestic life (200). Like Max Ebhart, Eddie is homeless and 'did need to be mothered' (278). He may also be a cad, but the abrasive edges which characterise Max and even Markie Linkwater are softened here. The result is a male character who reveals how men and women are damaged by sexual codes defined by domestic life.

The softening of Eddie's character represents the anomalous position of male character in domestic space. Once responsible for encoding patriarchal authority in domestic traditions, male characters could be made to serve its codes wisely, benevolently, like Jane Austen's Mr Knightly or Ray Forrestier. Representative of the end of this line, Thomas' authority is relegated to a basement study, out of the way, with no real moral or emotional influence. He has been succeeded by a wife who, like her mother-in-law before her, is made to wield a power in which there is no satisfaction and which sends weakened men into exile. To consolidate the damage to both male and female character, Bowen makes Eddie and Portia 'dreadful twins', caught in a state between manhood and womanhood, between the inscription of an Edenic domestic ideal and a fall into the betrayals of domestic codes (95). The narrator elaborates:

> Innocence so constantly finds itself in a false position that inwardly innocent people learn to be disingenuous. Finding no language in which to speak in their own terms, they resign themselves to being translated imperfectly. They exist alone; when they try to enter into relations they compromise falsifyingly – through desire to impart and to feel warmth. The system of our affections is too corrupt for them. They are bound to blunder, then to be told they cheat. In love, the sweetness and violence they have to offer involves a thousand betrayals for the less innocent. Incurable strangers to the world, they never cease to exact a heroic happiness. Their singleness, their ruthlessness, their one continuous wish makes them bound to be cruel, and to suffer cruelty. The innocent are so few that two of them seldom meet – when they do meet, their victims lie strewn all round. (106)

The lack of 'language in which to speak in their own terms' suggests an impasse between 'these two accomplices' and the world of domestic codes. They 'cheat' and betray those who feel protected by these codes from seeing themselves in Eddie and Portia (212). For as they impose their presence on 'The World', they challenge the Quaynes and the Heccombs to see that like Eddie, 'the whole of [them] isn't there for anybody' (214). Where Portia wants the world to support her desire to become whole, Eddie needs it to help him remain amorphous. Chameleon-like, he resists being 'piece[d]' into something that is not there, a character defined solely by defensive strategies like his various hosts (198). For Eddie, to remain formless, to be 'translated incorrectly', is safe because he then appears to satisfy everyone's expectations. In his way he saves himself and Portia from becoming the Quaynes: 'We don't want to eat each other. . . . like Anna and Thomas' (212).

Thus, Eddie's 'interior', his rooms, represent 'not simply the living here . . . but the getting away with it, even making it pay. He was able to make this room . . . a special factor, even the key factor in his relations with fastidious people' (278). His rooms reflect not only his defensive strategies, but the failure of others. Eddie 'hideous hired furniture' betrays the impoverished characters of Anna and Thomas as they are reflected in his 'animal suspiciousness, his bleakness, [and] the underlying morality of his class' (278). That he cannot afford to be 'a man-about-town in a Bourget novel' only testifies to the meagre use the upper middle class can make of him. This is a domestic novel where the traditional clash between the sexual aggression of the cad and the ordering power of family ideology is shown to be an anachronism. Eddie is really no threat to Windsor Terrace or to Waikiki; the cad has been housebroken by the erosion of passion in domestic space.

The logical consequences of an enervated patriarchal code are played out in Portia's odyssey after she runs away from the Quaynes. As she seeks refuge in Eddie's rooms, it becomes clear why these two cannot connect. At a stage where identity formation is most turbulent, the adolescent Portia, searching for sustenance in romantic love, finds herself in the wrong plot with a character inadequate to the challenge: 'she gave the impression of being someone who, having lost his way in a book or mistaken its whole import, has to go back and start from the beginning again' (277). In their last meeting at his flat, Eddie reveals to Portia how her demands dislodge the character he has tried to invent for himself. Her expectation that nurture will be part of sexuality moves Eddie to reveal how the domestic novel flattens male character:

> You apply the same hopeless judgments to simply everything – for instance, because I said I loved you, you expect me to be as sweet to you as your mother. You're damned lucky to have someone even as innocent as I am. . . . (281)

The wholeness and energy which Portia invests in a male character has no place in a domestic plot where nurture and sexuality are split between women and men.

Thus, Major Brutt's hotel, like Eddie's rooms, reveals how male character has no place to roost once the family home no longer encodes patriarchal power. Unmanned by the dismemberment of the empire, the major is as deracinated as his hotel: 'a class doomed from the start, without natural privilege, without grace. . . . even when they were homes, no intimate life can have flowered inside these walls or become endeared to them' (285). The loss of a battleground and rejection by Anna means that two settings which have honoured male character render him a lost child, another 'innocent'. When Portia tells Major Brutt 'you and I are the same', she groups him with all those who have been betrayed by and ejected from the family hearth (288).

Portia's quest for self-definition focuses ultimately on what it means to create and interpret the character of a woman. Her study of Mrs Heccomb's portrait of Anna as a child prefigures writing and reading as processes by which female character comes into being. When Portia first tries to decipher Anna's character from the portrait, she dreams 'she was sharing a book with a little girl', that 'she no longer knew how to read' (140). Later, Portia sees the 'little suffering Anna' representing an

'urgent soul astray', a female character floating painfully
among equally unsatisfactory plots (206–207). Portia reads
a shared experience into Anna's portrait: 'Inside everyone,
is there an anxious person who stands to hesitate in an
empty room? . . . not know[ing] what to do next or where
to turn' (141). For Anna, as for Portia, domestic space is
devoid of possibilities for fulfilment. The book they share
inscribes a plot which provokes anxiety because it does not
produce the 'ordinary life' promised by the 'airy vivacious
house' Anna has designed (42). Instead of being propelled
by the development of character, the book they share is
deterministic. No matter that Anna decorates her house to
suit herself; it conforms to a plot which inscribes a code
that ignores her needs. Likewise, Portia seems doomed to
dismissal by old patriarchal drama:

> . . . she was like one of those children in an Elizabethan
> play who are led on, led off, hardly speak and are known
> to be bound for some tragic fate which will be told in a
> line; they do not appear again; their existence, their point
> of view has had, throughout, an unreality. (297–298)

The remainder of the novel charts Portia's struggle to
enforce the 'point of view' of a developing character, to
bring her on stage once again. For Bowen this imperative
is most appropriately articulated by her fictional male
novelist, a plotter who upholds the right to decide the fates
of characters according to the canon he represents. Anna
asks her friend, the novelist, St Quentin Miller, for advice
when Portia runs away. Although he recognises that Portia
has 'a point of view', it is in terms which use traditional
metaphysics to dismiss it: 'Her "right thing" is an absolute
of some sort, and absolutes only exist in feeling' (308). St
Quentin implicates himself in Portia's effort to plot her
own course by telling her that Anna has read her diary.
Believing in the kind of inevitability that seems to allow

character to act out the consequences of their behaviour, he feels 'relieved to find how little guilty he felt' at his own plotting and for this reason, 'he loathed his renewed complicity' with the failed plots of Portia's adopted family (299,300).

With the introduction of this male novelist, Bowen's work establishes an opposition between a patriarchal tradition of character and plot and one in a tentative phase of experiment – Portia's diary. Acknowledging that Portia's diary 'put[s] constructions on things', St Quentin charges: 'you are a most dangerous girl' (250). The depth of feeling she invests in her writing, her lack of detachment, suggests a different kind of writer, not 'God's spy', as St Quentin calls her, but one who uses writing for self-discovery, to make 'connexions' so as to understand the role of other characters and of the past in her life (250,249). Bowen elaborates a view of writing that coordinates St Quentin's anxieties with Portia's hopefulness:

> We shall be confronted, at every turn, by means to express and complete ourselves – but how if, writers who can no longer write, we falter more every day at the sight of the blank white page. . . . have we lost illusion. . . . If so, it must be for the illusion that we hope to rifle the past. . . . We cannot hear enough, apparently, about childhoods – provided those are set more than 40 years back . . . the trivialities of yesterday have become our literature'.[5]

For St Quentin, writing is 'my game from the start', an imaginative construct which he controls, allowing him to 'swallow some lies' in order to 'carry the past' (249). St Quentin edits memory in order to transform reality into a tolerable fiction. The only character whose home is not even mentioned, he creates a safe haven in his art, as he explains to Portia: 'What makes you think us wicked is simply our little way of keeping ourselves going' (252).

Bowen's intense concern with the relationship between the fates of writers and those of characters and readers is evident in her narrator's statement early in the novel:

> Writers find themselves constantly face to face with persons who expect to make free with them, and St Quentin . . . detested intimacy, which, so far, had brought him nothing but pain. From this dread of exposure came his tendencies to . . . misunderstand perversely. (13)

Using a diary to explore the consequences of writing allows Bowen to highlight the betrayal inevitable to a writer's self-exposure. Thus, when St Quentin tells Portia that Anna has read her diary, Portia throws him 'a look like a trapped, horrified bird's' (248). Her book reveals, through what her readers bring to it, not the inner core of her being, but an interpretation of it. Unlike St Quentin, her unselfconscious style betrays the writer while exposing her subject.

The fear of being formed and exposed by reading and writing surfaces in Portia's relationship with Eddie. He, too, is a writer. While writing for a newspaper, he composes a novel which satirises his friends, making him a spy and traitor. He also writes letters to Anna that 'seemed blameless', but whose 'open writing [is] so childish as to be sinister' (61,72). Despite his efforts to compose himself, Eddie depends on Portia to create his character as a record of having mattered to someone. She will give him the substance he fails to create. Having tea at Mme Tussaud's, another world which interprets character, Eddie tells Portia that without her acceptance of him he would 'stay unreal for ever' (99). Yet her diary threatens him:

I hate writing; I hate art – there's always something
else there. I won't have you choosing words about me.
If you ever start that, your diary will become a horrible
trap, and I shan't feel safe with you any more (109).

Portia's writing proves to be his undoing, exposing him
as unable to compose a satisfying character. Implicit in
the writer's 'point of view', therefore, is the idea that
because the writer selects and edits what matters to him or
to her, it distorts and judges character even as it pretends
to verisimilitude. What makes Portia's writing riskier to
character and to writer than St Quentin's is her expectation
that character possesses as much feeling as she invests in it.
She creates character without a sense of where she ends and
the other begins. For St Quentin, there is so much distance
between writer, character and reader that there is no risk.
   Bowen's portrait of Eddie suggests that he has not
been able to affirm his character through any convention of
composing or interpretation in the fictions available to him.
Conforming to his interpretation of what others want from
him, he loses what little sense of himself he has. He makes
the mistake of yielding to the seductive promise of being
made whole by others taking up his character and moulding
it to their plots. Portia fails him because she cannot help but
shape his character to satisfy her need to make meaning
through writing. On his last day in Seale, Eddie describes
for Portia the consequences of projecting the writer's needs
onto the creation of character: 'In that full sense you want
me I don't exist' (214). Eddie is a male character dislocated
between fictional versions of himself and Portia's revisions
of the conventions he has chosen. She would remake the
'innocent' cad into a nurturant lover. Neither one can
'be happy with the truth . . . however small it was', or
with their respective versions of that truth (214). Neither
comforting fictions nor relative truths can compensate for
the emptiness characterising their relation to a world whose

conventions obliterate them. Failing to establish a safe place for his chameleon-like self, Eddie disintegrates into drunken tears on his last night in Seale.

Portia, on the other hand, is prepared to reshape the world until it conforms to her needs. The young author fills the silences and boundaries between herself and others with written language. Where Leopold reads other people's letters to find out how they control his life, Portia writes a diary in which she creates, selects and arranges the meaning of her experiences as she participates in the world of adults. The younger child finally learns about himself through the narration of his mother's life. Without a mother, Portia writes her own narrative, suffering through her moral and psychological education almost entirely alone. Her narrative is limited, but it expresses her personal discovery of the parameters of the world Bowen creates for her. In her writing Portia constructs causal relationships in people's lives, making out of her need for love a document in which she creates a place for herself in the lives of others, just as she did in her relation to Eddie and with Thomas. This is, after all, her book. Although, as St Quentin implies, books are to be read, the diary is so close to the writer's experience, Portia uses it to fill the empty spaces in her life, feeling free to be the self she is in the process of creating.

Writing also becomes a weapon, reshaping and diminishing those who fail to validate and sustain the self. Bowen felt this consequence of writing throughout her career. Recalling an early experience at Downe School, she finds it a way of wresting her life away from the lessons of others: 'I was taught not only how not to write, but how not, if possible, to behave, and how not to exhibit feeling'.[6] Through Portia's diary, Bowen asks whether it is possible to create a world of meaning by writing about it and what effect such an effort has on its subject and readers.

The novel begins with Portia's diary already having precipitated a crisis between herself and Anna. The novel is thus propelled by working out a connection between two alienated female characters through reading and writing. Interestingly, neither the passages reproduced from the diary nor Anna's statements about it indicate what produced her horrified reaction. Whatever it is, therefore, exists as an open space in the novel, suggesting that Portia's development into a writer requires her mastery of domestic conventions before she can give Anna substance in her book. Such a lack, corroborated by the narrator, implies that Anna's 'sexless and stiff' exterior and 'hollow' inner self can only be revised by a female writer creating a female character. Anna's efforts to shape herself within a traditional plot has led her, as St Quentin sees so clearly, to 'wr[i]te herself down' with a 'kind of bluffing' easily misinterpreted by an unsympathetic writer or reader (8). Anna sees the diary's method as 'distorted', but St Quentin confirms that after all, its function is 'to please oneself' (10–11). Through the diary, therefore, the novel raises a provocative question by dramatising the creative process which transforms people into characters in a domestic fiction. Are they merely pawns of the writer and the conventions available to her?

Portia's diary is a record of mostly prosaic events, about school and posting letters; it records only indirectly, through parenthetical comments, her impressions or feelings about what she sees. Through her cryptic asides, however, Portia reveals that her fundamental needs and their effect on those she watches, defy convention. In her entry for one Tuesday she reports a 'sort of' conversation she has with Thomas which occurs mostly 'by mistake' (112). Despite his nervous jokes about their father 'being caught', bitter references to love, and obvious discomfort at being caught alone with Portia, Thomas has no effect on an argument she constructs for the primacy of their relationship: 'After all he and I have our Father. Though he and Anna have got that thing together, there is not the same thing inside him and Anna, like that same thing inside him and me' (113). Portia's writing reshapes conventional distinctions between sexual and family relations.

Portia's revision of family structures positions Anna at the centre of her quest. The result threatens the older woman's defensive strategies: 'Well, she'll never find any answers here. . . . Who are we to have her questions brought here' (246). But Anna's ability to ask herself questions is necessary to the resolution of Portia's search. As 'The Devil' section develops, Anna and Portia become more closely identified, until Anna looks at Portia empathetically and their conflicting activities of reading and writing are reconciled. Only then is Portia given a share in the adult world and Anna a stake in the world of developing female character. Anna's moment of recognition occurs on returning home from vacation: 'Poor child . . . she stood about like an angel. It was we who were not adequate. . . . We all create situations each other can't live up to, then break our hearts at them because they don't' (239–240).

Shifting to an interior view of Anna's consciousness, the narrator establishes sympathy with her:

[Anna] knew how foolish a person looking out of a window appears from the outside of a house – as though waiting for something from the outside world. A face at the window for no reason is a face that should have a thumb in its mouth: there is something only-childish about it. Or, if the face is not foolish it is threatening – blotted white by the darkness inside the room it suggests a malignant power. Would Portia and Thomas think she had been spying on them? (244)

The passage coordinates and revises the novel's major tropes. The act of spying and the anxious expectant child who threatens the world of adults are images which now create an empathetic tie between Anna and

Portia. Recalling the portrait of Anna as a child, this passage situates Anna in the dual role of being and seeing the needy but threatening child and being a withholding mother-figure. The 'malignant power' resides in both figures: the insatiable expectations of the child for unconditional nurture and the resistance of a woman who has chosen not to mother. What Anna has seen in Portia's diary is the 'situation' neither she nor Portia can 'live up to' and which pits her needs for autonomy against her ward's need for dependence. Portia's diary, the discourse of the discovery of herself in relation to the mothers and spaces which have created her, is the key to the novel's interpretive strategy. Like any quest for self-definition, it must reflect and be answerable to the traditions of which it is a part. This work brings together the resisting mother in the role of reader and the needy child as writer to explore what kinds of female characters this creative and interpretive interaction will produce. The woman who will not mother, who creates an unsupportive domestic space, discovers that choosing not to is tantamount to self-denial, not self-determination. The adolescent girl who clings to maternal nurture cannot recognise the possibility of female character except as mother or as dependent child. The novel's solution is to have Anna and Portia deliver each other from their mutual but conflicted needs.

Once Anna identifies with Portia, she becomes the only plotter able to attempt a reconciliation; a model of the woman writer who designs domestic fictions which invite women to be autonomous and also empathetic. Asked how she would feel if she were Portia, Anna replies:

Contempt for the pack of us, who muddled our own lives, then stopped me from living mine. . . . Wish to have my own innings. . . . Frantic, frantic desire to be handled with feeling, and, at the same time, to be let alone. (312)

The experience of reading Portia's diary has moved Anna
to see her deprivation in the child. St Quentin asks: 'This
is all quite new, Anna. How much is the diary, how much
is you?' (312). Like Ray Forrestier, Anna understands that
her response to a child's demand for rescue and revision is
only a tenuous move toward change. But unlike the earlier
novel, this one casts a female character who resists paralysis
by assuming the judgement and responsibility formerly
attributed only to father-figures. It is no coincidence that
Anna's next statement appropriates Ray's mental state:
'Though she and I may wish to make a new start, we
hardly shall, I'm afraid. I shall always insult her; she will
always persecute me . . . ' (312–313).

Anna decides to send Matchett to the rescue, placing a
conventionally subsidiary character in the role of mediating
agent between Anna and Portia, between the compassionate
narrator and Portia's painful quest, and between the past
that produced Portia's story and her unsettled present.
Matchett's position in the novel helps Portia direct her quest
away from the confusions of houses, puzzles and pictures to
the kind of self-reflection necessary for self-discovery. The
only person willing to get close to Portia, Matchett is not
only housekeeper, but keeper of the past. Like Portia, she
is a legacy from the elder Quaynes. She embodies a living
memory of the domestic melodrama which drove Portia's
mother and father into exile and provokes Portia into
reconstituting that past as a painful, not always idyllic,
memory. Matchett serves as a kind of editor, facilitating
the piecing together of a coherent narrative for Portia to deal
with. Her questions form the narrative strategy necessary to
recreate the memories constituting the story of a life and
to understand the events which make connections between
one life and another. But Matchett's questions also liberate
the unique story of an individual from the 'unnatural living
[that] runs in a family' (81). If Matchett does not know
where she is being taken at the end, she is wise to the

ways of 'The World, The Flesh, and The Devil'. Ending her stream of associations, she asserts her authority, taking hold of the door of the Karachi Hotel while the narrator expresses hopefulness in the coming of summer as 'the highest and fullness of living' (318). As the novel ends we are assured that Portia will return to a house where the inherited pain of an old domestic story will be revised by a woman who may be first discovering the possibilities for her own.

Bowen designs Portia's rite of passage as a composing process which establishes communion with female characters already shaped by old fictions. First asking questions, then watching and deciphering the language and conventions shaping the world of adult men and women, Portia finally discovers meaning and coherence by writing her own story and discovering the necessity of creating an empathetic female audience.

The traditionally realistic mode works in tandem with the resolution Bowen designs for this novel. A belief in change leads to imagining destinies for female characters that are neither pre-determined nor violent. In this novel, Bowen makes writing by a woman the focus of that process which instigates change by creating a fictive world that is knowable. She allows her female characters to discover its parameters and their own stories. Writing serves to mediate between the female hero and those human relations comprising her world. Organising her language to shape an understanding of her world works as a kind of safety valve for Portia, allowing her to idealise and 'demolish' people imaginatively until they learn to accommodate each other. She creates fictions characterising the world as safe because she can control it. Portia's struggle to piece together the conventions of domestic life is a way of learning the origins of responsibility, giving order to her life, earning adult status, and gaining some control over her fate. The reader witnesses Portia's efforts to understand the nature of betrayal in order to wrest her story from a pre-determined pattern, as the narrator tells us: 'The strongest compulsions we feel throughout life are no more than compulsions to repeat a pattern: the pattern is not of our own device' (169).

The pattern, which began with a domestic melodrama of betrayal, repeats itself in the Quaynes' rejection of Portia. The wrath of the first Mrs Quayne is sculpted in Anna's fierce withholding. If Anna's snobbery and silence make her an agent of Mrs Quayne's plot, perpetuating unfeeling 'family custom', she is fated to play out Mrs Quayne's plot until she can provoke her will to respond to Portia's. Only then will the perception of writing as a 'trap' be recognised as a self-defeating fiction. The real trap, people's defensive relations with each other, is undone only through empathy, as Anna shows. As empathy is translated into seeing character as separate but interdependent with oneself, as mutual recognition of different needs, the writer's method changes. The signifying power of the past, of patriarchal traditions represented by houses to represent self-definition, gives way to recording the action of a woman writer composing her story. In this way Bowen's realistic method deactivates the reliance on houses as strategies for self-preservation and demystifies them as determining structures. For as Portia writes and creates an audience, characters are able to interpret their lives in relation to others, not as determined by the unknowable behaviour and patriarchal codes felt in the atmosphere of a house and its history.

Through writing and writing about writing, Bowen works out the mysterious terrors haunting her characters in earlier works. In her next novel Bowen will concentrate on the confused world of war in which uprooted men and women struggle to find a story that gives coherence to the chaos they create themselves.

6 *The Heat of the Day*

Eleven years elapsed between the publication of *The Death of the Heart* and *The Heat of the Day*. Although Bowen had written the first five chapters of *The Heat of the Day* by mid-1944, she felt that the strain of 'that V-1 summer' would affect the quality of the novel (*VG* 187). Instead of continuing, she decided to finish a volume of short stories, *The Demon Lover*. As Glendinning reports, Bowen could not finish her seventh novel until the war was over because only then could she say: 'I suddenly feel I know a lot more than I did. I have got the hang of what I meant' (*VG* 187). Writing this novel challenged her in new and complex ways. She wrote to Charles Ritchie to whom it is dedicated, that its structure and tone made it 'The most difficult of all':

> Sometimes I think this novel may be a point-blank failure but I shall still be glad to have tried. I would not in the least mind if this were my last shot, if I never wrote anything else again.
>
> It presents every possible problem in the world. . . . much of what is still to be written must be point-blank melodrama. (*VG* 187–188)

Although *The Heat of the Day* sold more copies than any of Bowen's other novels, critics have always agreed that it is also her most difficult.[1] The novel certainly demonstrates that Bowen was taking artistic risks. The aggressive imagery in her letter shows a desire to stretch beyond her earlier efforts, risking 'failure' with 'a last shot'.

The Heat of the Day deals with themes that compelled Bowen's earlier work, but its war-time setting occasions

a new impetus and perspective to her methods and concerns. The war not only provides an appropriate setting
and subject for themes of betrayal, self-discovery, and
dispossession, but is viewed from the perspective of adults.
Unlike her previous novels, the characters do not struggle
against determining pasts and lack of self-expression. If
their speech is difficult, it does not reflect lack of
access to a language of self-discovery, but rather the
self-knowledge which produces a language expressing
defensive entropy. These people are fully responsible
for their own plots. Whatever personal betrayals or losses
they face they participate in, but with reverberations far
beyond individual family histories. Individual betrayal in
this novel parallels treason, where a nation is betrayed by
one of its soldiers. The story of Stella Rodney, her lover
the spy, Robert Kelway, and the counterspy, Harrison,
creates a web of personal and political betrayal. In this
time of historic crisis, these people betray themselves by
acquiescing to their own sense of fatality. Collectively, they
suggest the possibility that the society they perpetuate but
cannot revitalise may collapse from internal and external
danger. As a result, the myth of the ancestral home, which
was demystified in earlier works, now burns more widely:
as the mother-nation – England.

War not only uproots men and women in this novel, it
reveals their basic rootlessness. Although Bowen portrays
the profound sense of loss and dislocation in wartime,
she also depicts those who have given up the hope
of stability and purpose. Once optimistic about the
ability of middle-class England to reconcile traditional
family values with the discontents of modern life, by
1942 Bowen saw only 'the explosion of the illusion
that prestige, power, and permanence attaches to bulk
and weight'.[2] Of the relationship between history and
personal experience, she said: 'outwardly we accepted that
at this time individual destiny had to count for nothing;

inwardly, individual destiny became an obsession in every heart' (*Demon* 50).

The Heat of the Day strains from its attempts to render the experience of disorientation and ambiguity. Bowen described how 'self-expression in small ways stopped' in wartime: 'One cannot take things in. What was happening was out of all proportion to our facilities for knowing, thinking, and checking up' (*Demon* 49). The opaque and ambiguous language which narrates this war story undermines the interpretive strategies of both characters and readers.[3] Spying, the activity which drives this war story, is supposed to uncover secret information and overpower those being spied upon; successfully performed, it guarantees power for those who control an exclusive, encoded language and powerlessness for those who cannot find the key. The result of dramatising this activity is that readers, like the characters, are put in the difficult position of following a chase whose terms are ambiguous and whose solution is predicted from the start, but at the end has led nowhere. Viewed in this way, Harrison's pursuit of Kelway collapses because there is no key to a solution at the end of the chase. Yet this novel also shows that the events of war only feel real through the stories which interpret them.

Combining concerns with narrative epistemology and conventions of spy melodrama raises questions about reader expectations. How should we read a mystery story whose conventions promise a solution when we are also being asked to doubt the language of such a story? For we expect spy stories to ferret out traitors and decode secrets. Solutions to conventional mysteries are problematised, however, in *The Heat of the Day* as its characters are afflicted with a kind of verbal inertia. The novel suggests that the expression of private fears is either irrelevant or impossible in a world overwhelmed by external terror and where traditional interpretations do not work. In this novel a society built on carefully ordered boundaries, one that values privacy, discretion and moderation, reveals a 'fatalistic' sense of a 'clearsightedly helpless progress toward disaster' (134). As Bowen said of the wartime London which inspired some of her strongest fiction: 'the wall between the living and the living became less solid as the wall between the living and the dead thinned' (92). With blackouts and bombings, day becomes night, night becomes day; strangers shed their life stories 'as so much superfluous weight', while intimates betray secret lives and unexpected stories.

The breakdown between self and other, past and present, truth and treason, and between exhilaration and despair inspires feelings of dissolution and disorientation, as well as a momentary, radical 'complicity' (96). Of the novel's attempt to render this experience, Bowen wrote: 'It is not about blitzes, etc., but about the peculiar psychological climate of those years, and the problems set up in people's personal lives'.[4] In combinations of naturalistic detail and hallucinatory visions, as in the cafe scene where Stella and Harrison meet Louie Lewis, Bowen elides conventional distinctions between reality and fantasy, between responsibility and chance, and between continuity and transience. With this rendering, the language of conventional fictions becomes an inadequate tool of self-expression, frequently expressing only vague abstractions and disconnected thought. Language in this novel communicates only uncertainty. Thus, even the language of love becomes 'the reiteration of unanswerable questions' (275).

The few books and photos which represent Stella's permanent life, the way Harrison turns up from nowhere, and Kelway's hatred for his family home all convey a sense of dislocation that begins within character itself. But despite the symmetry of these three portrayals, the source of dislocation is the woman. Unlike women in Bowen's earlier work, Stella does not provide any home base other than an occasional invitation to her borrowed flat. Having 'come loose from her mooring', she is Bowen's first female character to have given up the idea of making a home or of feeling tied to tradition: 'life had supplied to her so far nothing so positive as the abandoned past' (115). Unlike Karen Michaelis, in conflict about her family home, or Anna Quayne, designing hers to suit her ambivalence, Stella accepts dispossession. This shift in the formation of female character questions traditional connections between women's prerogatives and social stability.

Although the war setting directs our attention to the tragedy of dispossession and loss, for Stella, these are gains. In fact, the state of dislocation becomes her home, compatible with her desire to live in and for the moment. Nothing about Stella, including her job at the Ministry of Information, makes her a stabilising presence in the theatre of war. Her job of decoding language, like her spoken language, provides no firm information regarding her personal and political dilemmas. Indeed, the portrayal of Stella is a major factor in the novel's difficulty for readers. Yet despite, or indeed because of her elusiveness, what we come to see as her absence within presence, Stella is the novel's centre. Kelway and Harrison thrive on uncertainty only so long as Stella is there to provide some sort of emotional and epistemological anchor. Both spy and counterspy need Stella to make sense of their plots and their actions. But ambivalent to the end, uncertain in her commitments, she seems to sustain only the novel's mystery.

Stella's elusiveness derives in large measure from the novel's concern with language.[5] At forty, suffering the ravages of the blitz, Stella is first discovering what her character is really like. As she manoeuvres in and around her relationships with Kelway and Harrison, she questions the language of absolutes on which the social and literary traditions which shaped her are based. In turn, she is the means by which the male characters test the meaning of such traditional constructs as home, identity and moral responsibility. Gliding easily between worlds of treason and patriotic duty, she is pursued by the British counterespionage agent, Harrison, who looks to her for the true story about her lover, suspected of spying for the Nazis. Although Kelway does collaborate with the enemy, his treachery seems authentic and real only as Stella is involved in interpreting it. As Harrison pursues her more relentlessly than he does her treasonous lover, Bowen's narrative transforms a traditional male genre into a female-centred plot. Making Kelway's guilt a given allows Bowen to focus on the more difficult task of questioning assumptions about women's roles in stories about the personal dimensions of national peril. She extends our expectations of spy thrillers to explore the relationship between the language of secret stories and the hidden selves of women. Each man brings his plot to Stella for interpretation, all the while fearing that she will either withold its meaning or that the meaning she holds within her may cause their dissolution. In a war story where interpretation seems impossible, the woman is suspected of harbouring secret meaning. Stella's elusiveness turns out to be her protection from the spy plot which, if she became involved, would cast her in its presumed moral dichotomies. As she becomes the focus of the spy plot, the meaning of power, of the language of absolutes, and that of identity itself, become as elusive as her character.

Stella's position undermines the distinctions which make spy stories possible. Only through Stella's involvement with both men do we learn that they share the same first name, Robert, a sign that Kelway is interchangeable with his nemesis, Harrison. Just like 'the man from nowhere' who cancels himself out by speaking only in double negatives and becomes 'a ghost or actor', a 'face with a gate behind it', Kelway uses a language which cancels his individuality, indeed, which leads to his disappearance into the chaos he fears (141,12). His death, either by 'fall or leap', confirms the failure of language to construct absolute boundaries of difference. He disappears from the narrative in ambiguity.

Harrison seems to have no identity or story at all, except as his pursuit of Kelway establishes a relation to Stella. He is only palpable through the story of Kelway's treason and Stella's ambivalence towards him. Louie Lewis knows him by sight, not by name, and Donovan, the estate manager at Mount Morris, can remember him only by the wrong name. In search of a story in which he can play a part, 'he was as a character "impossible" – each time [he and Stella] met, for instance, he showed no shred or trace of having been continuous since they last met' (141). The triangular relationship of Kelway, Stella and Harrison undercuts the conventional moral distinctions of male character in spy stories by refusing to exploit melodramatic interpretations of female character.

At this mid-point in her career, Bowen implicates both historical event and historical fictions in her formation of female character. Her self-consciousness about narrative forms effects a view of female character which is distanced by many references to books and stories, as well as by the narrator's meditations on history, time, reality and destiny. But unlike much post-modern fiction, *The Heat of the Day* acknowledges the reality of historical event and its moral dimension, even as it undercuts traditional moral polarities and views history through the relative visions of psychological defences. Such countermoves are designed to unsettle our conventional responses to female character as they make her the locus of the novel's ambiguity.

In *The Heat of the Day* war exposes the instability of conventional moral dualities. Distinctions between 'good guys' and bad break down and all clues become canards as every meeting between Harrison or Kelway with Stella diffuses the meaning of personal and political loyalties, indeed, explodes the representation and definition of spying itself. As Stella tells Harrison, 'you *are* a counterspy, which I understand to be some sort of spy twice over . . . ' and then at their next meeting, 'Below one level, everybody's horribly alike. You succeed in making a spy of me' (39,138). Bowen is not using Stella's remark to mock the moral distinctions necessary to fight Nazi Germany. Rather she is questioning the notion of difference itself, especially in readers' expectations of how male and female character embody different spheres of responsibility.

Despite their frantic reliance on a rhetoric of absolutes to make sense of their actions and plotting, spy and counterspy enact the futility of such language to provide an interpretive key – to the meaning of their characters, to that of the woman they assign the role of decoder, or to their lack of a sustaining homeland. Thus Kelway justifies his treason to Stella by equating 'freedom' with a 'slave's yammer' and betrayal with a language of 'dead currency' (268–269). This is a language of undecipherable noise; it provokes such anxiety that it moves men to yearn for unbreakable law, unambiguous order. Kelway's complaint is linked to his home – Holme Dene – which resembles Danielstown or the house in Paris as a labyrinth of 'repressions, doubts, fears, subterfuges and fibs', all controlled by a mother (256). Like the war itself, Holme Dene fosters 'creeping and spying'; its sense of order betrays an inherent disorder. A 'man-eating house', it threatens to incorporate its inhabitants (257). But suburban Tudor Holme Dene is only a parody of an ancestral estate or haunted house. Therefore, Kelway's indictment of its disturbing atmosphere as representative of his society's failures seems both an empty and overstated justification of his treachery:

> I was born wounded: my father's son. Dunkirk was waiting there in us – what a race! A class without a middle, a race without a country. Unwhole. Never earthed in . . . (272).

Kelway's treason merely substitutes one set of abstractions for another; 'order' for 'freedom'. Such a rhetorical and

interpretive strategy allows him to equate his home-
land/Holme Dene with a fascist order, but readers of
Bowen's earlier work will recognise the danger signal
in any plea for order as a cure for what ails a society.
In Kelway's case, the battle cry for order is doubly
problematic. On the one hand, his treason is shown in
part to enact a rebellion against his mother's castrating
domination. Wounded at Dunkirk, his limp is compared to
a 'stammer'. This 'psychic' wound makes him inarticulate,
like all those characters in Bowen's fiction who suffer the
silence of a controlling maternal regime (90). At the same
time, however, he can be seen to identify with his mother
by favouring the enemy who does not just give orders, but
'means order' and 'silence' (273). But like her home, Mrs
Kelway parodies a tradition. To be sure, the woman her
son calls 'muttikins' is controlling and withholding. But
her manner and her son's relation to her draw attention to a
cardboard figure who, in the face of world-wide destruction,
can no longer be made to embody some kind of supranatural
evil power. The vision of her knitting while London burns
suggests Mme De Farge as farce.

Debunking a maternal monster problematises Kelway's
character, for Bowen's indictment of oppressive order now
focuses on the son. That his rhetoric slips easily into
destructive politics is implicit in an assumption Bowen
could make about her readers in 1949 and after: we
know that the new 'order' institutionalised a myth of
difference, of a racial hygiene that might save Kelway
from the 'hated . . . bloodstream of the crowds, the curious
animal psychic oneness', but would result in a holocaust of
unimaginable dimensions (275). Kelway's version of Nazi
Germany leads the reader to translate his abstractions into
concrete historic events, an exercise which makes his rhetoric of self-justification more deadly than any image of the
mother as monster. The cad re-emerges here in a new form.
His role in romantic melodrama no longer disguises his real

motive, which is to use sexual and political power to save his enfeebled character from extinction. Kelway's reliance on his lover to save him only highlights his peril. Stella's playing for time, allowing Kelway to prove his innocence or guilt on his own, without her help, shows that he is the source of his own danger. He is imperilled, not by any lack of order in his inherited culture or by the frustrated power of women, but by his particular use of the language he inherits from his patriarchal forebears. He interprets the abstractions which serve as hallmarks of any cultural order as absolute ends in themselves, so that the language of broad philosophical flexibility becomes an absolute weapon of destruction. As he speaks, Kelway retreats into silence, becoming as unpalpable as the abstractions on which he bases his life.

As personal history and political history are woven into mystifying stories, Kelway's betrayal and the roles played by Harrison and Stella become interdependent. The texture of their relationship shatters conventional definitions of loyalty and guilt. It does so by situating female character at the centre of a spy story, reversing our expectations of a conventional genre which usually places female characters on the periphery – as Mata Hari figures subsidiary to the superspy or as the angel of the hearth waiting in the wings to be the spoils of men's valour, honour and righteousness. Stella's character questions such characterisations. She refuses to participate in any moral self-congratulation while also insisting that moral fables falsify women's experience in war. Faced with accepting Harrison's proposition to sleep with him and save Kelway or discovering Kelway's guilt or innocence, Stella vacillates. She accepts the position of being morally questionable in order to avoid sharing Harrison's responsibility for Kelway's continuing treason and participating in a plot which replicates the story of Kelway's betrayal.

Kelway's use of Stella to restore belief in him coincides

with her 'holiday from fear' (90). Together, they succeed in creating only a 'phantasmagoric' world which replicates the dispossession, betrayal and loss each feels with a 'despairing hallucinatory clearness' (91,93). The vision of a suspended, nightmarish perception of reality expresses Bowen's interpretation of a protective state of mind during wartime. As she noted in the preface to her wartime stories, 'The hallucinations are an unconscious, instinctive, saving resort on the part of the characters: life, mechanised by the controls of wartime, and emotionally torn and impoverished by changes, had to complete itself in some other way' (*Demon* 49). Such a defensive strategy requires a guarded if not opaque language designed to avoid the horrors exposed by war; it does not ask questions or make specific references to the war's events. The strangely abstract quality of the lovers' language approximates the loss of a sense of concrete reality. Stella's affair with Kelway is described in this way:

> Most first words have the nature of being trifling: theirs from having been lost began to have the significance of a lost clue. What they next said, what they said instead, they forgot: there are questions which if not asked at the start are not asked later; so those they never did ask (96).

Imposing a kind of 'muteness' on themselves suspends Stella and Kelway in a romantic tale which seems to keep the empty, silent and brutalising conditions of war at bay. But history seeps into their relationship just as the searchlights and the glare of crashing bombs come through their drawn curtains (126). Instead of saving themselves, the lovers foster mutual suspicion as they refuse to use language to explore the meaning of the present, to clarify their characters to each other, or to plan for a future. The 'poetic sense of order' with which they seek to protect themselves is composed in a problematic discourse which only imprisons

Stella and Kelway in a solipsistic story of betrayal they create for themselves (90). From the beginning, precisely because we are introduced to Kelway's treason and his affair with Stella through her encounter with the nebulous Harrison, their story seems fated to cancel itself out, as Stella's self-fulfilling vision attests: 'She saw Robert's face . . . certain that he was dead' (93). Placing their relationship on 'the borderline of fiction' questions the historic reality of the plots which enfold them (97). 'Vacuum as to future was offset by vacuum as to past'; this narrative cannot identify a particular historic moment, but only a continuum of undifferentiated dread, where polar opposites, such as war and peace, become fused (95).

Stella, however, both participates in this fiction and is set apart from it. She is fully aware of the duplicitous and unstable nature of stories and interpretation, as in the one about her divorce. Like Kelway's treason and Harrison's counterespionage, the end of Stella's marriage to Victor Rodney is not dramatised, but narrated as a man's story. Like that of Kelway and Harrison, its language of polarities threatens to destroy its subject. This narrative is particularly dangerous to female character. As Stella tries to save her marriage and to interpret her husband's story, she cannot find a way to assert the authenticity of her feeling. Her character is lost in Victor Rodney's belief in an ideal, absolute dimension of feeling. Telling her husband that she loves him is proof to him that she does not because he feels that she cannot 'have the remotest conception of what love was' (223). Just as Stella is betrayed by Kelway's rhetoric and Harrison's reliance on the language of war to sort out the 'crooks' and 'put the other lot of us in the right', so she is overwhelmed by her husband's insistence on a language of absolute definition which betrays her relative experience (34,33).

Unable to fathom why Victor wanted a divorce, Stella encourages belief in a different story: that he gallantly allowed her to divorce him because she had a lover waiting in the wings. Preferring to be characterised as a 'monster' rather than a 'fool', Stella uses Victor's story as a passive-aggressive strategy, one that conceals her character while inventing one (224). The power of absolute definition to remain stable is subverted by a woman imposing her own fiction. She uses Kelway and Harrison in the same way. As she divides her allegiances between them, she protects herself from the treachery of believing in permanence and continuity by perpetuating a story of continuing elusiveness. It is for this reason that Stella leaves Harrison to prove Kelway's treason, helping neither one until she realises her lover is in danger. Her tolerance of other people's stories, however, combined with her fiction-making, only reinforces suspicions that she is corrupt.

Stella's past reveals that war did not make language tentative and duplicitous, but that war stories by women writers reveal the danger in relying on the literalness of language.[6] Language fails as a vehicle for self-discovery because war exacerbates a pre-existent condition. 'The habit of guardedness' reinforces 'an existing bent' in Stella; 'she never had asked much, from dislike of being in turn asked' (26). Stella is threatening to her husband because he suspects that although she would like the meaning of language and life to coincide, she does not trust it to as he does: 'Having been married by Victor, having had Roderick like anyone else, made me think I *might* know where I was' (224). Like her husband, Kelway cannot depend on Stella to acquiesce to his plot. Her need to interpret his story in the light of her experience, to revise his reality through her own story-telling, may translate into interpreting his spy story as a sham. Hence he sees Stella's questions as an 'immaterial, crazy thriller' which 'seeds itself in some crack' between them, 'locked up inside' her, but 'always being taken out and looked at' (190,191). The combination of his metaphors equates her attempts to figure him out with an hysterical pregnancy, a story that is beyond control. She carries the seeds of his life and death within her as a mystery whose clues are unfathomable to him.

That Stella is suspected of powers she does not possess is confirmed by Harrison's pursuit and abandonment of her. As elusive as Stella, he is none the less dependent on her to provide a story in which his character can be stabilised. He may feel at home in Stella's flat and 'touched' by the story of her past, but that is only because these things have 'come to matter too little, having mattered too much' to her (226,229). Precisely because Harrison's cynicism confirms her own distrust of abstract principles does she consider sleeping with him. What matters to her at this point is that she can save the lover she has jeopardised. Our attention to Kelway's treason and Harrison's role in exposing him is overshadowed by the novel's insistence that both men and indeed the narrative itself, are more concerned with Stella and her elusive story than with the spy and his secrets. In a world where efforts to interpret reality collapse into hallucinatory chases without resolution, the mythic image of woman as possessor of secret knowledge re-emerges. Just as Kelway suspected, because she is unknowable, this woman seems to embody the secret all their spying is after: the power to affirm their plots in her inaccessible story, even if *she* has not found the key.

Through Stella's vacillations between personal loyalty and expediency, Bowen questions traditional assumptions about women being the key to moral stability. Stella confuses Harrison by acquiescing to him in a way he has to refuse. But in so doing, she saves herself from his dependence on her and dooms spy and counterspy to the logical consequences of their own plots. Stella thus is left to stand as a model of apartness, impervious to brands of honour which promise only to dishonour her

developing sense of herself. Central to a story which turns
on world-shattering historic events, she represents female
character in flux; she cannot be pinned down to any moral
definition or convention. Stella's position reflects that of a
female character caught between three deadly alternatives
the novel questions. It comes across as a kind of cynical
passivity, but represents the powerlessness of other women
in the novel.

> After all, one can only live how one can; one generally
> finds there is only one one *can* live – and that often
> must mean disappointing the dead. They had no idea
> how it would be for us. If they still had to live, who
> knows that they might not have disappointed themselves
> (88).

The dead and the near dead in this novel are other women:
those in the portraits at Mount Morris, the Irish country
estate Stella's son inherits, and Cousin Nettie, confined to
a rest-home for the insane. Both reflect back on the position
of female character in worlds that appear to be stable but
are about to blow up.

Stella's visit to Mount Morris illustrates Bowen's complex
feelings about the relationship between women's character
and the end of the family home. What Stella sees and feels
there connects war-torn England, a decaying Irish big
house, and the position of female character in stories that
have become as moribund as the societies which produce
them. A picture in the drawing room of Mount Morris of
the Titanic going down 'in a blaze of all lights on' recalls
the burning of Danielstown in *The Last September* as well
as Stella's London (176). The picture belongs to Nettie
Morris, related to Stella through marriage, and marks
their connection as the last of 'this society of ghosts'
where 'Ladies had gone not quite mad . . . from in vain
listening for meaning in the loudening ticking of the clock'

(174). Like Stella and Nettie, these Anglo-Irish women were passive in their 'knowledge of unspoken terrors'; what 'they suspected they refused to prove' (174). The implications of Stella's kinship with the isolated and powerless women of her son's patriarchal ancestry are contained in the history of Cousin Nettie.

Although the reasons for Nettie's self-imposed exile remain ambiguous, signs emerge from Roderick's visit to her that her story and Stella's derive from the myth of the ancestral home. Nettie's 'madness' actually enables her to look beyond 'the surface' but like the ghostly ladies of the big house, she is afraid of 'divining what should remain hidden' (207). Mourning for the man who should have remained her cousin, not her husband, Nettie flees into madness from an inbred marriage which is symptomatic of the claustrophobia and isolation Stella feels in the drawing room of Mount Morris. Nettie's only purpose in Anglo-Ireland was doomed to failure: she did not produce an heir. She tells Roderick: 'Who knows what might not have come of a different story, if there could have been one. As it was, he had to go out looking for a son' (209). Nettie's story is about a wife who abandons her inherited purpose: perpetuating the legend of family continuity and tending the self-destructive order of Anglo-Ireland. Stella's story parallels Nettie's. In giving up the idea of making a home, Stella abandons the purpose of women of her class. Stella's cynical passivity, Nettie's madness, and the female ghosts of Mount Morris position the concerns of a domestic novel within a spy story, a narrative move which shows that the apparently dissimilar quests of these genres focus on the same need for maternal presence. Stella's elusive presence stands for a woman's betrayal of her inherited role. She abandons the homestead to transform women's buried stories or mysteries: that 'her own life should be a chapter missing from this book need not mean that the story was at an end' (175).

The power to correct the historical fiction of war stories and myths of family homes is left to the child of the enigmatic Stella and to a younger woman who searches for her own story. For Louie Lewis, the war represents the need to find a story that will give her stability and purpose. Alone and without a sense of herself since her parents died in the Battle of Britain and her husband left for the front, Louie turns to newspaper stories to discover a character with which to identify and feel whole. She discovers, however, that other people's language and stories are discordant with their behaviour. The fact that Stella 'spoke beautifully' does not accord with the impression that she 'walked like a soul astray' (245,248). When the story of Kelway's death and involvement with Stella appears, Louie feels 'infected' by 'unununderstandable languages' (247,248). In a world where other people's absolute and closed fictions have wrought havoc, Louie creates her open-ended and ambiguous story. She uses the telegram announcing her husband's death to invent a father for her illegitimate child and returns to her home town to provide him with a heritage.

Louie's presence in the novel functions as a countermove to the spy story and to a retreat into either madness or cynical passivity. That she is Bowen's one major working-class character reflects a new perspective. Glendinning reports: 'Psychologically, one of the results of the war for Elizabeth was the breakdown of boundaries and barriers. . . . "Life with the lid on" was over for good, and a lifetime's policy of "not noticing" increasingly hard to maintain' (*VG* 177). The genteel constraints on behaviour before the war became irrelevant at a time when those who stayed behind in London enjoyed intimacies with people they might never before have met, sharing intense feelings openly and with relish. Bowen wrote of her experience: 'I would not have missed being in London throughout the war for anything: it was the most interesting period of my life' (*VG* 158).

Louie has been viewed by most critics as a vital alternative to Stella's passivity.[7] But like her upper-class acquaintance, Louie is trapped inside a story she cannot fathom and is displaced from her origins. Dispossession robs Louie of her sense of adulthood so that 'having been left with no place to go to', in a somnolent state, 'she almost always returned with sensual closeness to seaside childhood' (16,17). Louie's 'infant' perceptions lead her to project her need onto the external world, erasing distinctions between different times and people (17). One result is that all the men she sleeps with are versions of her husband Tom because her only 'censor' and sense of 'certainty' reside in her memory of him (15).

War not only deprives Louie of home and a sense of self, but of an intimacy independent of articulation. She is left in a double bind, having to maintain contact through verbal communication when she has no natural form of self-expression to give her a sense that 'she, Louie, *was*. . . . From on and on like this not being able to say, I seem to get to be nothing, now there's no one' (15,245). After meeting Stella, she tries to explain to her friend Connie how lacking a verbal outlet for her feelings makes her feel engorged with unexpressed language:

It's the taking and taking up of me on the part of everyone when I have no words. Often you say the advantage I should be at if I could speak grammar; but it's not only that. Look the trouble there is when I have to only say what I *can* say, and so cannot ever say what it is really. Inside me, it's like being crowded to death – more and more of it all getting into me. I could more bear it if I could only say. (245)

Without language Louie requires 'someone to imitate', a way of creating a place for herself in a story with which to identify. But such an effort makes it impossible for her to discover her own story as distinguished from others. Like Stella, Louie comes to terms with the way history determines character and the way our own fictions are undermined by other forms of self-creating stories. We are given no reason to believe that the fiction Louie invents to give herself and her child identity will help them in a world where fictions have proved to be the source of its potential destruction.

If Stella proves that either resisting fiction-making or continuous invention cannot undo history, her son Roderick will risk rebuilding the 'fatal connexion between the past and future' by restoring his father's ancestral home and traditions, that is, if he survives the war (176). Stella's reaction to Mount Morris, however, confirms that this solution is problematic. As she leaves her son to his 'green world of the past' and leaves the narrative as well, Bowen leaves him to the fate of a traditional plot she critiques. The only language available to men to rebuild their civilisation is that which signified its destruction by first driving its women into 'deep silence' (175). Stella's identification with the portraits of women driven 'not quite mad' is countered by Louie's retreat from identifying with Stella into a fiction of beginning life anew.

Rather than cancel each other out, as Kelway and Harrison do, Stella and Louie represent the future of possibilities for female character. As representative of the class Bowen had explored in all her previous work, Stella is made to save herself at the cost of uninvolvement with traditional fictions and values. Being homeless no longer prefigures tragic determination. Bowen's statements about her own experience during the war combined with the fate of the character who is her own age at this historic moment suggests an interesting celebration of the end of a kind of oppression. For like the burning of Danielstown, which left its heroine free to leave Anglo-Ireland for an unknown destiny, Bowen here blows up the last vestiges of upper middle-class family homes. Stella is older and perhaps has fewer options than Lois Farquar, but the parallel disappearance of both women at a time of historic crisis suggests that only disturbances in cultural stability can provide opportunities for a way out of conventional fictions and imagined fates for female characters.

If Bowen does not write a utopian fiction, she creates imaginative states of mind for her female characters to have them play the role of critical historians of the past. So in her next two novels, *A World of Love* and *The Little Girls*, her female characters return imaginatively to the past to decipher its meaning for what has happened to them since. The betraying past in *A World of Love* is revealed through a pack of letters. But the writing in these letters is not an act of self-expression of discovery; it is a sign that the past must be treated with sad, if bemused, tolerance. No one is made to suffer or to show responsibility for betrayal. Whatever self-discovery the young heroine, Jane Danby, makes through identifying with the letter-writer and her lover is undercut by Bowen's parodic portrait of the lover as ghostly libertine. At the end the letters burn quietly, having never explained, restored, or resolved the past.

The Little Girls confronts the intersection of ageing, the failure of imaginative fictions for self-discovery, and coming to terms with the past. In some ways it is a sad story, reflecting Bowen's personal odyssey in the last years of her life in which she seemed to encircle her own past. Yet this novel also contains some of her most sharply critical and comic moments. It is as though the sense of tragedy and ironic perspectives

which clarify her greatest concerns have been understood
and absorbed into a creative gesture which expresses
affectionate distance from the relationships and histories
which had compelled her creative imagination for fifty
years.

7 Elizabeth Bowen's Fiction

The apparent choices of art are nothing but additions, predispositions: where did these come from, how were they formed? The aesthetic is nothing but a return to images that will allow nothing to take their place; the aesthetic is nothing but an attempt to disguise and glorify the enforced return. All susceptibility belongs to the age of magic, the Eden where fact and fiction were the same: the imaginative writer was the imaginative child, who relied for life upon being lied to – and how, now is he to separate the lies from his consciousness of life? If he be a novelist, all his psychology is merely a new parade of the old mythology. We have relied on our childhoods, on the sensations of childhood, because we mistake vividness for purity; actually, the story was there first – one is forced to see that it was the story that apparelled everything in celestial light.[1]

The appearance of two biographies of Elizabeth Bowen and the reissue of her novels, short stories and family chronicle, *Bowen's Court*, have been greeted with considerable enthusiasm. Yet recent appraisals mirror the conflicted opinions critics have always expressed about Bowen's place in literary history. Most critics agree that she is a consolidator of 'modern comedies of manners', who connects a line from Virginia Woolf to that of Iris Murdoch and Muriel Spark (*VG* XV).[2] Bowen's themes and subjects are usually placed in the English realist tradition of Jane Austen, George Eliot, E.M. Forster, and Henry James.[3] But for those who emphasise Bowen's portrayal of intense emotion, she is a novelist of sensibility.[4] This appraisal also takes two directions. Her use of houses as symbols of psychological oppression reminds readers of the gothic and romance fiction of the Brontës while she is also identified with the modernism of D.H. Lawrence since she defines her characters by their states of feeling.

Attempts to make her fit the traditions of the English novel say more about canon formation than they do about Bowen's work. In Hermione Lee's view, 'Elizabeth Bowen is an exceptional English novelist because she fuses two traditions – that of Anglo-Irish literature and history, and that of a European modernism indebted to Flaubert and to James' (11–12). Victoria Glendinning has suggested that her 'original inimitable voice' captures cultural dislocation and personal loss so pointedly and poignantly only because she is a transitional figure (*VG* V). As feminist scholars point out, however, viewing a woman writer as a connecting link in a primarily patriarchal tradition diminishes and conceals what is exceptional about her work.

In their recognition of literary traditions of women writers, feminist scholars and critics provide an opportunity to read Bowen differently. These readers have explored the unique contributions of women writers within the social, religious, political and psychological contexts which shaped their individual creative consciousness. Identifying the narrative strategies and voices which emerge from these contexts places women writers in traditions of their own. As Showalter and Gilbert and Gubar have shown, we can now see women writers not as slipping between one patriarchal tradition and another by writing in their margins, but as marginalised people who show their understanding of 'The Great Tradition' by critiquing it and revising it as 'a literature of their own'.

Bowen is a marginalised figure in several ways that are transformed imaginatively into a distinctive style and persona. Neither English nor Irish, she was born Anglo-Irish, an uneasy identity in both cultures. She was the last heir of a 'big house', one of those country estates built in Ireland in the eighteenth century by members of the Protestant Ascendancy that was a source of power and prestige until civil war threatened its physical and political foundations. Unlike her patriarchal forebears, however, Bowen assumed responsibilities which afforded her little more than a vacation site and the heartache of an economic burden. As a writer she was also accustomed to not belonging. With her first publication in 1923, she resisted the intellectual headiness of Bloomsbury and comforting conventions of the Galsworthy-Bennett tradition, preferring instead to read them and to learn, and to create a form of her own. Balancing her Anglo-Irish landed heritage and being a successful writer, she manoeuvred between worlds which usually did not meet. Her artistry reflects the tension of such balance in portraying people always on the edge of belonging anywhere. Like her characters, Bowen and her work resist classification. When her fiction is assessed according to traditional literary categories, it is criticised for being excessive, for having a convoluted prose style, obscure references and abstract dialogue, as well as for reflecting the anachronistic views of a 'conservative with nostalgic temperament'.[5]

Exploring Bowen's fiction within the context of her marginality enables us to see her both as a British novelist and standing apart from its traditions. For she is a critic of those social and literary forces which shaped her work. In her comedies of manners she not only questions the morals of country and city life, but those literary traditions which reflect, express and prefigure them: romance elements and domestic realism are never taken at face value. Rather, her sensibility transforms social comedy and sentimentality to show the acute psychological states which underlie and result from the social codes which shape her drawing room encounters. Readers generally connect Bowen's social comedy and romance by synthesising them into a theme of disenchantment, relying on her oft quoted statement: 'It is not only our fate but our business to lose innocence, and once we have lost that it is futile to attempt a picnic in Eden'.[6]

Most interpretations of this definitive statement overlook the tendentiousness of Bowen's reference to 'Eden'. If we view Bowen's work as a response to the literary history of themes of disenchantment as well as to her appraisal of social and political experience, we can see her critical and creative artistry coalesce. For Bowen's characters may enact a pervasive theme in the English novel, but they also reflect the disenchantment of Irish civil war in the twenties, the threat of worldwide upheaval in the thirties and forties, and post-World War II apathy. The experience of Bowen's characters actually questions the assumptions and consequences of the literary and social traditions to which they owe their lives. Lost innocence in Bowen's work is an idea which belongs both to the literary traditions in which she writes and to her personal and cultural experience. Her characters' acute psychological states are particularly compelling because they are double-edged. They live within extreme states of consciousness – hysteria, fear, loss, deprivation and rage – and they respond not only to the human relationships in which Bowen places them, but to the cultural and literary contexts in which she conceives them.

Bowen has often been compared to Henry James, particularly to his elaborately nuanced portrayals of the moral and psychological shape of lost innocence. Portia Quayne in *The Death of the Heart* or Leopold in *The House in Paris* could be cousins of James's Maisie, all children damaged by the sexual worlds of adults. Bowen's fiction takes us inside the conflicted relations of parents and children, showing us their origins in the ambivalent desires of both. Her narrators are never effaced or dispassionate as in James. They are always partial and involved, positioned at the centre of the narrative, indeed, advocates of the characters. In this way Bowen's narrators frequently resemble those of George Eliot in their expressed sympathy for her characters' suffering. But once again, Bowen gets closer to her characters than Eliot and James do to theirs. For more than sympathy, Bowen's narratives enact empathy. In *The House in Paris* the narrator identifies Leopold's suffering with a list of cataclysmic world events. In *To the North*, the narrator presents and interprets Markie's shocked response to Emmeline's sexuality with imagery which expresses Markie's feelings. In *The Last September* Laurence is shown to identify with his long-dead aunt Laura's feelings about her life at Danielstown.

Bowen's desire to merge her narrators' consciousness with the experience of her characters reflects a stance that is critical as well as empathetic. Often, as in Leopold's case, the narrator feels deeply both for the child and for the characters who may stand in opposition to him. Bowen's response here is to the narrative traditions she shares with Eliot and James, but it also reflects her position as outsider both culturally and as a woman of her time. At the same time that her narrative voice empathises with that of her characters, it finds a form of expression that reflects the politics of mother-child relationships amidst time-honoured literary, psychological and social conventions. Bowen's fiction glosses the intellectualised liberal and humanist views of her predecessors. Thinking of her own work as she reviews Ivy Compton-Burnett's, she shows them both responding to the literary traditions they inherited. Bowen and Compton-Burnett express the raw emotion drawing-room manners could no longer conceal:

What then, was this task the Victorians failed to finish and that the Edwardians declined to regard as theirs? A survey of emotion as an aggressive force, and account of the battle for power that goes on in every unit of English middle-class life.[7]

Bowen's critics have observed that her themes of dispossession and loss which are expressed with intense feeling derive from her ambivalent responses to her marginalised childhood experience.[8] Howard Moss observes that being 'English in Ireland and Irish in England, [Bowen] grasped early the colonial mentality from both sides, and saw how, in the end, it was a mirror of the most exploitative relationship of all: that of adult and child' (128). In one sense Bowen's concerns are thus personal and cultural, while in another, they are literary. They are framed in what Gilbert and Gubar have shown to be the struggle of women writers with their literary forebears to find voices of their own.

Bowen's personal, cultural and literary legacies inform her portrayals of characters caught between ties to inherited traditions and their desire to upset them. Her childhood in an Anglo-Irish big house made her understand how family tradition creates a place which promises identity and purpose, but which also controls one's destiny and suggests, in its forms of living, conflicting messages: 'its intense, centripetal life isolated by something very much more lasting than the physical fact of space: the isolation is innate; it is an affair of origin' (*BC* 20). Bowen often creates children who are made to suffer the conflicts of family relations as they are symbolised by family homes. The intensity of life in a family home seems to promise infinite nurture while its isolation marks a sense of being left out; it signifies the secrecy which defines boundaries between the worlds of adults and children. Her adolescent and adult protagonists suffer the residual scars of childhood or remain needy children even as adults. They face the fragility or break-up of the family while their expectations of love and security are betrayed. They rebel against family constraints yet yearn for its intimacy. Karen Michaelis in

The House in Paris experiences herself as her mother's child even after she makes the rebellious decision to love someone who will never be welcome in her family's home. Edward Tilney in *Friends and Relations* enacts his childhood suffering in his adult passions while Portia Quayne in *The Death of the Heart* yearns for and yet challenges the family home designed to reject her.

The interdependence of children and adults, of inherited traditions and rebellion, focuses on the omnipresence of the past. As a creative inspiration for Bowen, it becomes a living presence in her work. The power of the past assumes its importance in the family's ability to preserve its traditional forms so that it can perpetuate itself. The process of maturity that Bowen's characters endure consists of giving up the childhood wish for reconciliation and union with the mythical nurture and order of the family home and past. It is a process that requires one to adjust selective and romanticised memories to accommodate the pain of disorder in order to learn that identity lies in a jaundiced appraisal of the past.

In her essay 'The Bend Back' Bowen asserts that looking to 'one's past: childhood, [for] the better days', is like reading fiction, illusory and comforting, and therefore dangerous. Yet 'one invests one's identity *in* one's memory. To re-live any moment, acutely, is to be made certain that one not only was but is'.[9] The past is recapitulated or restored through memory, but memory is as deceptive as the past it invokes and as the way we read stories: 'Intrinsically, the appeal of the past is moral – here are displayed, in action, virtues of boldness we had dreaded to lose. In responding to them, the reader, with gladness, feels the stir of something dormant within himself' (*BB* 224). Bowen's protagonists go through a process of demystifying their pasts. They must learn to see how the past is distorted by psychic and social necessity and by those people tied to the purpose of perpetuating the order and traditions they

associate with the past. The power of the past lies in its
psychological and moral claims. Its inherited responsibilities
are shown to have dubious value only as they are revealed
to be part of a process of mythologising the past. Nowhere
is this more apparent than in Bowen's Irish novel, *The Last
September*, where the myth of the big house dominates and
is destroyed. As it haunts Bowen's imaginative memory, the
Irish past is always present in her fiction:

> The past of Ireland is an uneasy subject: controversial,
> bloody and bitter, with no trappings, few uninterruptedly
> pleasant prospects down which the eye can run. To the
> English mind, that past is not even stirring – it is too full
> of defeats. The tragedy is too plain to permit analysis –
> and it is for analysis, inference or the picturesque that
> history is read now, as an exercise or another kind of
> escape. Peace-lovers seek the past because it is safely
> over – and nothing in Ireland is ever over.[10]

She links the theme of the past to her understanding
of Anglo-Irish psychology: 'In Ireland, if you do not
know the past you only know the half of anyone's
mind'.[11]

In Bowen's creative imagination the past is coterminous
with places; together, they pervade every aspect of her
themes and structures:

> The influence of environment is the most lasting . . . and
> operates deepest down. Sometimes, the force of environ-
> ment may be felt by a writer's conscious, sharp reaction
> against it. Admittedly, it is the atmosphere of the scenes
> of youth which is most often decisive – though it has
> happened that, some way on into life, a writer has
> stumbled upon a place, perhaps an entire country, which
> he in some way recognises, which seems to claim him,
> and which offers a hitherto lacking inspiration to his art.

In that case, there is a sort of psychological adoption: a new phase of freshness of feeling, equivalent to a second childhood, sets in. But the majority are haunted by the shadowy, half-remembered landscape of early days: impressions and feeling formed there and then underly language, dictate choices of imagery. In writing, what is poetically spontaneous, what is most inimitably individual, has this source – the writer carries about in him an inner environment which is constant; though which also, as time goes on, tends to become more and more subjective.[12]

In her case, of course, the past and places come together as the big house in her Anglo-Irish background. Describing these big houses in *Bowen's Court*, she conceives of them and their inhabitants as being inextricably bound to each other so that past and present, isolation and suffocation are experienced as sensations emanating from the house itself: 'Character is printed on every hour, as on the houses and demesne features themselves. With buildings, as with faces, there are moments when the forceful mystery of the inner being appears' (*BC* 20). In this sense the house seems to absorb the lives of those it has sheltered and contained.

As Hermione Lee has observed, the works of Maria Edgeworth and Sheridan Le Fanu represent the Anglo-Irish side of Bowen's literary influences. In her review of Le Fanu's *Uncle Silas*, Bowen compares this 'romance of terror' to *Wuthering Heights* in its 'pressure, volume and spirited urgency'.[13]

The hermetic solitude and the autocracy of the great country house, the demonic power of the family myth, fatalism, feudalism, and the "ascendancy" outlook are accepted facts of life for the race of hybrids from which Le Fanu sprang.

This reading shows how Bowen and Le Fanu share an Anglo-Irish heritage and the sense that family homes are determining structures for her characters. Effecting a causal relationship between character and house, Bowen, like Le Fanu, uses the 'atmosphere' of a house to depict both the strictures and emotion which family homes represent to her repressed characters but which they are often unable to express. Houses represent a 'heightening of conflict in [characters] between hopes and fears, rather than the melodrama of [their] approaching fates . . . (*US* 6). From the literary heritage of Le Fanu and from Edgeworth, Bowen develops a 'psychological thriller', where 'because of [their] upbringing, [characters] . . . move about in a world of strangers . . . (*US* 7). Thus Stella Rodney in *The Heat of the Day* wanders through the Anglo-Irish big house her son has inherited, frightened by the sense of foreboding that she may become one of the portraits of ghostly women who lived and died there.

In many of Bowen's short stories, houses haunt the living, appearing to be characters in their own right. In turn, houses reflect the characters' ambivalent feelings; they are haunted by the empty promises of ever-lasting privilege as well as by ghosts of those who either failed to fulfil those promises or who suffered the responsibilities of privilege without experiencing its power. In the story 'Foothold', the new owner of a Georgian house is haunted by a 'sickening loneliness' projected by the ghost of a previous owner (*CS* 313). In 'The Back Drawing Room', an English visitor to Ireland after the time of the Troubles discovers a woman weeping in a big house left unaccountably open. Without any sensory sign, he experiences vivid fear and danger 'like the House of Usher', as though transmitted by a weeping woman who expresses the subsequent fate of the house (*CS* 209). Haunted by the scene, the visitor discovers that the house was burned two years earlier. The messages emanating from the life-like structures which haunt the living are mixed and mysterious. Windows seem to stare and also to reflect; a hall can wear 'an air of outrage' and walls can absorb and/or radiate warmth and frigidity (*CS* 386). Younger people, like Lois and Laurence in *The Last September* or Roderick Rodney in *The Heat of the Day* have great difficulty unravelling and deciphering the messages houses seem to represent. They feel that if only they could find the essential life of the house, they could locate its power and make it their own.

All of Bowen's protagonists, children and adults, attribute the contradictions and failed promises of their fates to real, imagined or unattainable family homes. Bowen designs their quests for origins, purpose and expression as an attachment to the idea of home. Cumulatively, homes in her work assume mythic proportion for her characters. Houses represent more specific experiences than suggested by their use in the English novel as symbols of confinement or female inner space.

For Bowen's characters, houses are nurturing but dominating, ordered worlds which suppress violence. For while houses suggest the solidity of tradition, their foundations are shaken by the pressure of lives within, leading either to 'decompression or to explosion' (*BC* 453). Bowen's assessment of life in the Anglo-Irish big house becomes her characters' disappointed expectations in all dwellings: 'Lives in these houses, for generations, have been lived at high pitch . . . in psychological closeness to one another and under the rule of the family myth' (*BC* 19).

In all of Bowen's writing houses exert a power over characters' lives that is felt as a mutually dependent and demanding relationship. Born dispossessed, both young and adults are frequently powerless to determine their own destinies; they project their wishes for cultural and personal identity, power and support onto a fantasy of an ancestral family home. As it emerges in Bowen's work, the ancestral home becomes encased in a myth, a story purporting to explain the past and provide solace in the present. Hence her characters pursue stories of the past, looking for the intentions of their ancestors as though that would explain their present chaos. Bowen's view of selfhood was shaped by a felt need to transform the unstable forms of family and home into a language and story that could be trusted.[14] As her plots repeatedly show, however, the myth does neither. Its language, which seems to promise the power of discovery and expression, is riddled, contradictory, and as it belongs to a problematic past, is useless to Bowen's characters. They must discover that the past provides neither stability nor sustenance, and they must therefore contend with the fact that history has rendered claims of inherited power inoperative and inconsequential. The myth thus includes the seeds for a revolution which will destroy it and the home on which it is based.

Representative of inherited privilege, houses in Bowen's fiction embody the social, moral and even legal codes of their particular society. House and codes alike are designed by the men who built them, but it is the women, such as Lady Naylor in *The Last September* and Mrs Michaelis and Mme Fisher in *The House in Paris*, who are given the dubious power to manage them and the lives they contain. This social and political framework is given a psychological perspective by Bowen's compelling focus on the emotional lives of the women and children who inhabit family homes. In turn, families themselves are often represented as holding environments, so that houses and families become metaphors for each other. Because the primary province of women is the family home, houses and mother-figures come to signify each other's best and worst interests. Empowered to control, but powerless to imagine pursuits outside the family structure, Bowen's women are marginalised characters in these novels of self-discovery.

In this light, we can interpret Bowen's statement about picnics in Eden as being more radical than she has been given credit for. When Bowen's female characters lose their innocence, they understand that picnics are women's work, part of their preordained role in a domestic space that was never a paradise. Bowen's female characters enact the consequences of the arrested development prescribed by English domestic fiction for women. To see Bowen's work in this perspective does not represent an argument that she should be considered a feminist writer. Indeed, she dismissed such labelling, as when she questioned the feminism of Virginia Woolf as an 'obsession' that became 'a bleak quality, an aggressive streak, which can but irritate . . . '.[15] Despite this dismissal, readers cannot ignore the persistence of female characters in Bowen's work who struggle with autonomy, dependence and self-expression in circumstances always defined by traditional family values. Bowen's statement that 'women effect necessary change' resonates in the struggles of her heroines.[16]

Bowen's empathy is reserved not only for children, but for those who are ordained to serve as their mothers. Once she moves away from the Irish setting in *The Last September*, she transforms her feelings about children's isolation and intense family relationships into the upper middle-class world of London and the English countryside. Here it becomes more apparent that women endure their assigned domestic and maternal roles in suffering that appears as silence or emotional paralysis. In these worlds children are not the only ones who feel isolated from knowing what determines their fates. Women, too, like Karen Michaelis and Emmeline Summers, enact their prescribed social roles, sometimes like somnambulists, going through the motions, but showing little understanding of why they are fulfilling them. Integral parts of family and social structures, they are none the less alone. Laurel Tilney and Janet Studdard in *Friends and Relations* are sisters who love and trust each other and who have a mother who understands and cares about them. Yet they behave as though they are isolated on an emotional desert island. They have no guides to show them how they should react and respond to the challenges to their emotionally charged lives.

In these portrayals, Bowen responds to the tradition of the *femme seule*.[17] Despite different social and economic contexts, Bowen's female characters are drawn with concerns shared by the Brontës, Jean Rhys and Katherine Mansfield. What Bowen gets and reworks from these writers is the intensity of their frustrated desires to find self-definition and expression in emotionally impoverished worlds. Unlike the compromised or tragic resolutions George Eliot imagined for Dorothea Brooke and Maggie Tulliver, Bowen's women are rarely offered the possibility of reconciliation in life or in death. Even where reconciliation is held out as a strong possibility, as between Karen Michaelis and her abandoned son or between Anna and Portia Quayne, it never takes place. Indeed, the violent ending of her last novel, *Eva Trout*, shows an irreconcilable gulf between mother and child, as well as between a woman's frustrated desire for self-expression and the possibility for achieving it.

If Bowen's heroines are not isolated by economic and social position, they experience isolation in the face of traditions represented by the homes in which they live or, as in the case of Eva Trout, by the alienation from any possibility of home. Bowen's empathy for children's feelings of abandonment and loss are complemented by her portraits of their mothers. These women are trapped in maternal and sexual roles they may have chosen, but in which fulfilment and self-expression are always compromised by social expectations. The pleas of children such as Leopold and Portia for nurturing homes are answered by the questions or silences of Karen and Anna who fear the costs of motherhood to their sense of themselves. Bowen's female characters are also isolated in the sexual roles prescribed for them. From the sixteen-year-old Portia to the *ingénues* Sydney Warren and Emmeline Summers, and the sophisticated women in their thirties and forties, Anna Quayne and Stella Rodney, women in Bowen's fiction are expected to welcome sexual relationships as validation of their womanhood. Yet each one is clearly ambivalent, showing both a yearning for intimacy and a fear of violation by men shaped by patriarchal codes which prescribe women's responses and roles.

Bowen reveals the consequences to female character of literary traditions which have cast women in roles of the *femme fatale* or of mother. Male anxiety and fear of women's sexuality have been replayed in literature from ancient times. But closer to Bowen's cultural heritage, D.H. Lawrence presented both the fear and a defence against it. Gudrun Brangwen in *Women in Love* is the apotheosis of the sexually devouring woman, while her sister Ursula is capable of transforming her demands for autonomy and independence into the 'star equilibrium' which allows her lover Birkin to feel assured that she will no longer be a threat to his own needs. Bowen's creation of the sexually enticing Emmeline Summers, the budding *ingénue* Portia, and the enigmatic Stella Rodney shows how female character is threatened by a literary tradition which insists that a woman's sexuality is dangerous. Plots which appear on the surface to promote romantic union between a man and a woman actually stereotype female character, erasing all the ambiguity that evokes complexity in female desire and casting her instead as a monster. Bowen's portraits assert that a woman is more than her sexual attractiveness and her potential for motherhood. For Emmeline's sister-in-law, Cecilia, like Ursula Brangwen, chooses marriage as a solution to her still undefined needs, but Bowen makes it clear to her readers that more is lost than gained in such a solution. Cecilia will make a home, not only for her husband, but for his ward, whom she would have preferred to hold at arm'slength, as Anna does with Portia. At the centre of a family home, there is no space designated for Cecilia alone.

Although most critical attention has been paid to Bowen's child characters, the writer gives equal time to her adult women. Younger and older female characters represent the possibility of change as they seethe with rage against the domestic traditions which bind them. In her portrayals of adolescent sensibility, Bowen can easily be compared to her contemporary, Rosamond Lehmann, who showed women coming of age with anxieties that engulfed their sense of a sexual and intellectual self. Bowen's women always seek expression outside of sexual relationships. In *A World of Love*, sexual, romantic love appears only as a ghostly presence in the lives of the novel's four female protagonists. If Bowen's heroines never discover outlets other than being wives, lovers and mothers, they highlight the desire for them. Moral choices in Bowen's work are complicated by the presence of women's desires, which are viewed by others, often older mothers, such as Mrs Michaelis, as anarchic forces in rebellion against traditional morality. Thus Janet Tilney's decision to renounce her love for her sister's husband remains disquieting even as it restores domestic equilibrium. For her passion has clearly represented more than sexual frustration; it has called for a reassessment of what women's domestic imperatives mean to whatever is left to their lives. Family values in Bowen's fiction prevent women from feeling that their passions have a place in domestic space. Instead, their passions are inscribed in family homes which rock with the threat of their unleashed energy. Self-discovery is thus discovering the energy hidden by housekeeping and mothering and disguised by sexual passion.

Each woman in Bowen's work represents a powerful energy frustrated by domestic expectations. Even in the wake of social change wrought by World War I and the vote for women, Bowen feels the effects of a society clinging to traditional values. She herself managed her life with all the decorum necessary to live within a conservative world while manipulating its conventions to suit her personal desires. Her novelistic style mirrors her life. As the history of critical comment shows, she can easily be read as affirming a time-honoured credo of 'feeling strongly that a morally valuable innocence can be reconciled with a harsh will to self-assertion, that ideals of personal fulfilment somehow work in the world'.[18] Her deployment of decorum in staid and elegant drawing-rooms, however, actually challenges the ideology of manners. Instead of 'keeping the lid on', a phrase she used to describe the *modus operandi* of Jane Austen's world, she smashes it again and again, even while she shows the insistent presence of Jane Austen's world in her own. Thus her female characters both embody and rail against domestic codes which seemed to be at their most powerful in the Victorian period but which Bowen shows prevail even through the cataclysmic global upheaval of two world wars. Monica C. Fryckstedt defines the domestic ideology of the nineteenth-century English novel as that which 'glorified the values of family and home. [Its] emphasis [was] on submission to the will of God, fulfillment of duty, self-sacrifice, and endurance' (22). Bowen's mother-figures embody such a code since they are a 'peculiar combination of invisibility and vigilance' and thus 'represent the principle of domestic economy itself'.[19]

When Bowen's women find themselves ineluctably bound to domestic life, their passion for selfhood seems contained and constrained by a traditional plot which resists social and literary reform. Her female characters play out the role of moral and social manager while other elements in the novels' structures enact the women's frustration with tradition's resistance to change. It is for this reason that many of Bowen's realist plots contain elements of romance and the gothic. As Gubar and Gilbert argue, women writers split conventional romantic dilemmas and resolutions from expressions of anger and resistance in their techniques. In this way women writers skirt the mainstream of the English novel while subverting its ideologies. Bowen layers various narrative modes, all of which provide her with a technique to examine the development of female character in the British novel. We can see the expression of women's frustrated selfhood and their rage in characters like Mme Fisher in *The House in Paris* and Elfrida Tilney in *Friends and Relations*. Featured as disrupters of domestic order, they are opposed by prototypes of maternal stability – Mrs Michaelis or Laurel Tilney. Mme Fisher's character falls somewhere between Charlotte Brontë's Bertha Mason and Jean Rhys's. Seething with unexpressed passion and energy, Mme Fisher is confined to her bed – a prisoner of all the social and literary codes which have not availed her of an outlet. Elfrida Tilney has rebelled against being a wife, mother and even lover as she chooses to live alone. She is not unlike Mme Laure in Eliot's *Middlemarch*, leaving weakened and dead men in the wake of her passion; she is the result of being other than what is expected of her.

Although Bowen's female characters owe their frustration to patriarchal codes, men are never portrayed as villainous. They, too, are victimised by codes which they have no power to change. Men like Ray Forrestier in *The House in Paris* seem to be in charge, but just as he gives up his career as a diplomat to accommodate his wife's needs, so he concedes that his plan for a reconciliation between mother and child is no panacea. Men are not heroes in Bowen's fiction. They are weakened by the lack of psychological, social or political authority. Even where they are economically successful, the luxuries they can afford are no compensation for the emptiness and lack of direction and purpose they feel. Thus Richard Naylor dreams only of being besieged in his big house by Irish rebels and Markie Linkwater's success as a barrister only signifies a rather myopic vision of the real conflicts and adversaries which threaten him. Bowen's male characters cannot facilitate the changes necessary to empower the women they love or save themselves from the women who threaten them. They are portrayed as essentially apart from women in a kind of 'stand-off', holding their fears of impotence at bay.

Bowen's recognition of the literary expression of women's frustrated energy goes back to her childhood reading of Rider Haggard's novel *She*. In her BBC broadcast about the books which had affected her deeply, she recalls:

> At the age of twelve I was finding the world too small: it appeared to me like a dull, trim back garden, in which only trivial games could be played. . . . Hemmed in by what seemed to be too much safety, I felt bored and hampered . . . Worse still, I had exhausted the myths of childhood.[20]

In Haggard's outsized 'She-who-must-be-obeyed', Bowen found an image of an avenging female angel whose powers of self-expression are unleashed and expressed.

> *She* contained thoughts and sayings I never had seen in print, and certainly never had heard spoken. . . . What her powers were I knew and I could not doubt that she would exercise them to the full. . . . This book *She* is for me historic – it stands for the first totally violent impact I ever received from print. . . . Writing – that creaking, pedantic, obtrusive, arch, prudish, opaque overworded *writing* . . . what it could do! That was the revelation; that was the power in the cave. The power whose inequality dear Holly [the hero] laments at the opening of every passage. The power of the pen. The inventive pen. (*She* 113)

Bowen's inventive pen takes up the cause of *She* by revising and extending the myths of her childhood. Like *She*, Bowen 'break[s] loose and avenge[s her]self for the long centuries of solitude' of women (*She* 112). Combining the methods of fairy tales with the realism of myths in domestic novels, Bowen gives expression to women's pent-up energies.

Bowen's sense of domestic ideology is expressed as a shared system of belief contained in the values permeating her characters' attitudes and behaviour, their social and intimate lives. With wry wit, she dramatises these values in the drawing-rooms of Cecilia Summers, Cecilia's Aunt Georgina, Anna Quayne and Mrs Michaelis, where arch gestures summarise and gently satirise a history of acceptable behaviour. But each of these settings and characters is explored critically by elements of intensified emotion and compressed or grotesque characterisations. In her pairing of female characters such as Mme Fisher and Mrs Michaelis or Cecilia and Emmeline Summers, Bowen questions traditional oppositions between motherhood and sexuality, and autonomy and dependence.

Bowen's use of opposition as a technique to question the formation of female character has its most dramatic expression in her treatment of houses. Every staid and elegant drawing-room in her novels is paired with houses which represent the lethal power of domestic codes. In its suggestions of claustrophobic oppression, the house in Paris stands in opposition to the more subdued control of the Michaelis home; Mount Morris in *The Heat of the Day* represents a peaceful contrast to war-torn London, but its atmosphere is threatening to Stella and all the women who have ever lived there. Bowen manipulates the meaning of houses as they have been transmitted through literary traditions. Her portraits of empty but claustrophobic houses challenge our stereotypical associations of family homes with a nurturing and beneficent female essence. In showing how women subvert and rebel against domestic codes, she charts a dangerous course for her career. In *The Last September*, she sets fire to the Big House so that we can understand the implications of domestic space for all the characters who have felt dependent on it. But its emotional associations are present in every house she portrays afterwards, thus calling into question any sense we have of a changing or progressively liberal composition of domestic space and its dictates for women.

The anxieties which accompany fantasies of claustro-phobic homes are conveyed by a technique associated with a sense of the visionary.[21] Bowen described the source of this sensation as 'a scene [which] burned itself into me, a building magnetised me, a mood or season of nature's penetrated me, history suddenly appeared to me in some tiny act or a face had begun to haunt me before I glanced at it' (*EBS* 78). The technique which translates this sensibility into literary image shares much with the work of Katherine Mansfield, which Bowen describes exactly as she does her own: 'She found herself seized upon by a scene, an isolated incident or a face which, something told her, must have meaning, though she had yet to divine what the meaning was. . . . It is a style generated by subject and tuned to mood'.[22] Although Bowen reports that she only read Mansfield's stories after publishing her own first collection, she feels encouraged by Mansfield's example: 'the idea and potential of "atmosphere" were accounted anew'.[23]

Bowen's psychological thrillers 'exploit the horror behind reality'.[24] Hermione Lee has explored Bowen's work as using psychological themes to analyse social reality in a liberal humanistic tradition of moral responsibility. But Bowen's ghosts and houses undermine that very tradition in which she works. Her use of language, which has been criticised as idiosyncratic, serves to unsettle the reader's reliance on conventional moral dualities. Her double nega-tives, unfinished sentences and arch use of abstractions are her post-modern response to moral complacency. Her syntax expresses doubt, not acquiescence, either to the moral or literary tradition in which she lives and works.

Her language expresses acute ambivalence or the inability
of conventional language to express the emotional paralysis
which results from ambivalence. In *The Last September* Lois
Farquar's final plea to Gerald Lesworth becomes the model
for Bowen's concern with language:

> It's like a nightmare that even you should begin to talk.
> I thought you were a rock: I was safe with you. Gerald,
> really, this is all like a net; little twists of conversation
> knotted together. One can't move, one doesn't know
> where one is. I really can't live at all if it has all got
> to be arranged. I tell you, even what I think isn't my
> own. . . . You don't know what it's like for a snail, being
> walked on. . . . (*TLS* 191)

Bowen's language represents a struggle for autonomy
in self-expression, and where her characters express their
inability to find a language of self-expression, Bowen's
imagery, her own deployment of language, expresses their
dilemmas. Thus in its complex of images and metaphors
the atmosphere of houses becomes an expressionistic device
offering a simulation of her characters' experience. This is
never more acute than in her last novel, *Eva Trout*, where
the heroine, who has inherited untold millions, cannot buy,
build or make a home in which she feels comfortable and
who cannot discover a language of self-expression. Her own
aphasia and dispossession are mirrored in the character of
her mute son whom she drags from one unsatisfactory place
to another. About to depart on a fake honeymoon, she
abandons her son, a turn of plot which she has designed to
restore or finish her character. But instead, Eva is finished
off by her child. As he shoots her, their combined rage
explodes in a place of transit. This no-place becomes an
emblem of the radical displacement and perhaps disgust
Bowen feels about both domestic plots and romance as
devices for forming female character. Clearly, for Bowen,

domestic space has been no Eden for Eva or any other female character.

Eva is gunned down as a failed mother and lover, heiress to a fortune that led nowhere. Although this last novel is problematic in many ways, its attenuated narrative, its extremes in characterisation and plot, illuminate what is particularly balanced in Bowen's revision of domestic and romance plots. Her portrayal of an inept and inexpressive woman shows how traditional narrative has silenced the woman who cannot or will not be a mother and lover. Bowen's story grants her heroine access to expression in a novel which stumbles on the effort. Bowen traces her concern with the language of female self-expression in the English novel to the work of Virginia Woolf. In a lecture to women students she allied herself to Woolf: 'It is more difficult for a woman to be a writer of action. She should concern herself with the link between the sensibility and the act'.[25] In *Eva Trout*, Bowen shows her link to Woolf's use of distanced inferiority. Bowen, however, pays greater attention to the lack of access to self-expression for female character. For her, women's inexpressiveness is a function of how their will is paralysed by social and literary traditions.

Bowen's tie with other British women writers enables us to re-evaluate her originality. Her experiments with language now have a thematic purpose and her treatment of women and children have a critical place in literary history. The surfaces and attitudes of her work are conservative only in the sense that she presents a world bound to tradition. But all her work serves as well to question and revise the ideological and social assumptions of all traditions.

Notes

Notes to Chapter 1

1. Elizabeth Bowen, 'Manners', Review of *Can I Help You?* by Viola Tree, 1937, *Collected Impressions* (New York: Knopf, 1950), p. 68.

2. 'Coming Home', *The Collected Stories of Elizabeth Bowen* (New York, Knopf, 1981), pp. 95–102. All further references to Bowen's short stories are cited in the text as *CS*.

3. 'Out of a Book' in *Collected Impressions*, p. 265.

4. Elizabeth Bowen, *Bowen's Court* (New York, Ecco, 1979), p. 451. All further references are cited in the text as *BC*.

5. Victoria Glendinning, *Elizabeth Bowen, A Biography* (New York, Knopf, 1978), p. 18. All further references are cited in the text as *VG*.

6. *Seven Winters: Memoirs of a Dublin Childhood* (London, Longmans, Green, 1943), p. 27. All further references are cited in the text as *SW*.

7. 'Origins' in *Pictures and Conversations* (New York, Knopf, 1975), p. 12.

8. 'Places' in *Pictures and Conversations*, p. 47.

9. Ibid, p. 53.

10. 'The Mulberry Tree', in *Collected Impressions*, p. 193.

11. *Why I Write* (London: Percival Marshall, 1948), p. 56. All further references are cited in the text as *Write*.

12. 'Preface to *Stories by Elizabeth Bowen*' in *Afterthought: Pieces about Writing* (London, Longmans, 1962), p. 77,80.

13. 'Sources of Influence' in *Afterthought*, p. 208. *Coming to London* ed. John Lehmann (London, Phoenix House, 1957), p. 77.

14. 'Preface to *Stories by Elizabeth Bowen*, pp. 77,78.

15. Letter to May Sarton, 5 October 1952, by permission of the Berg Collection, The New York Public Library.

Notes to Chapter 2

1. Elizabeth Bowen, 'The Big House', in *Collected Impressions*, p. 199. Future references will be cited in the text as *BH*.

2. In *Seven Winters* Bowen recalls that '[my] most endemic pride in my own country was . . . founded on a mistake: my failing . . . for

vowel sounds, and the Anglo-Irish slurred, hurried way of speaking made me take the words 'Ireland' and 'island' to be synonymous' (15).

3. Bowen writes in the essay 'Uncle Silas': 'Two things are terrible in childhood: helplessness (being in other people's power) and apprehension – the apprehension that something is being concealed from us because it is too bad to be told' in Collected Impressions, p. 15.

4. The metaphor of women's illness derives its impact from Bowen's family history: her father's mother died as a result of nursing his smallpox and Bowen's mother was seriously ill from pregnancy and the miscarriage of a second child; she died of cancer when Bowen was thirteen.

5. Edwin Kenney notes that Bowen is both adult author-narrator and Anglo-Irish only child, making 'patterns of her adolescent crises for her lonely characters', p. 37.

6. Allen Austin discusses Lois's identification with Danielstown, p. 41.

7. 'The Last September' in *Afterthought*, p. 6. Further references to this essay will be cited in the text as *P*. In her 'Preface to Stories by Elizabeth Bowen', she claims that 'places more often than faces have sparked off stories'; in an unpublished letter to Virginia Woolf, dated 26 August 1940, Bowen writes: 'But places are so very exciting: the only proper experience one has. I believe I may only write novels for the pleasure of saying where people are. And the advantage of short stories is that means a different place every time.' Berg Collection, New York Public Library.

Notes to Chapter 3

1. Elizabeth Bowen, 'Origins', in *Pictures and Conversations*, p. 2. In notes to a lecture on 'The Experience of Writing', (Wellesley College, 20 March, 1950) she describes *Friends and Relations* as her 'first "pure" novel' which 'arose from brooding over a face seen', p. 4, unpub. ms at Berg Collection, NY Public Library.

2. Bowen recalls that from the time she lived in Kent with her mother ' "History" inebriated me, and no wonder. Moreover, *here* was where it belonged: Kent-England had a proprietary hold on it' as opposed to Ireland, where 'history – because, I suppose, of its melancholy, uneasy trend – had on the whole tended to be played down; one knew *of* it, but spoke of it little', 'Origins' in *Pictures and Conversations*, p. 26,25.

3. *The House in Paris*, p. 70. Most critics have not liked *Friends and Relations*. See Austin, Heath and Kenney. Hermione Lee sees it as 'an evasive text which seems to resist interpretation by overinterpreting itself', about 'a large non-occurrence', p. 64–65.

4. 'Encounters' in *Afterthought*, p. 86.

5. In *Seven Winters* she describes her childhood incredulity at the idea

that a house can exist without a child's presence: 'A house where a child no longer is is virtually rolled up and put away', p. 7.

6. See Austin, p. 41.

7. See Kenney, who also sees the novel as static. Critics attribute flaws in *To the North* and *Friends and Relations* to their having been written in rapid succession, 1931 and 1932.

8. Patrick Brantlinger distinguishes the romance form as expressing wish-fulfilment fantasies.

9. See J.J. Bachofen, Wolfgang Lederer MD, Erich Neumann, Philip Slater, Sigmund Freud, 'Medusa's Head', and 'The Theme of Three Caskets'. Two prominent contemporary male artists who perpetuate this myth are: Robert Bly, 'I Came Out of the Mother Naked' in *Sleepers Joining Hands* (NY: Harper, 1973) and John Fowles, in *Mantissa* (Boston: Little, Brown, 1982), where a male artist is sexually assaulted by his female muse.

10. Paul Friedrich calls attention to the overdetermined linguistic, cultural and religious meanings attending the figure of Aphrodite as it informs mythological figures of women in the ancient and modern worlds.

11. See, among others, Mary R. Lefkowitz, Ada Farber, Karen Horney, Sarah Pomeroy, Ruth Moulton, Estelle Lauter.

12. See Sandra Gilbert, 'What Do Feminist Critics Want? A Postcard from the Volcano' for the theoretical context of this point.

13. See Jessica Benjamin, Nancy Chodorow, and Jane Flax, on the relation of women's sense of self and issues of fluid boundaries.

Notes to Chapter 4

1. Edwin J. Kenney discusses the novel's 'bold division', pp. 46,48.

2. Feminist scholars who study how maternal conflict affects women writers include Nancy Chodorow, Jane Flax, Judith Kegan Gardiner, Marianne Hirsch, Elizabeth Abel.

3. In a letter to Charles Ritchie, she wrote of *The House in Paris*:

> It really did impose itself in the most extraordinary way, like a sort of deep gripping dream. When I wrote it, it was much more like hunting for language and images which would most strongly transcribe something which had happened or which I already knew, and yet I myself had not been any one of the characters in the dream. . . . I don't feel I in any way invented or, as it were, devised 'The House in Paris,' which I suppose really is the ideal feeling to have about a book . . .
>
> (quoted in Victoria Glendinning, pp. 121–122)

4. See Michelle Barrett.

5. See Rachel Brownstein for her history of the cad as well as Lee R. Edwards.

6. See Jane Flax, 'Postmodernism and Gender Relations in Feminist Theory'.

7. Hall calls Max 'mother-ridden', p. 26. In *Bowen's Court* Bowen analyses Henry Bowen III who resembles Max, p. 127.

8. This quotation is omitted from the appropriate paragraph on p. 146 of the Penguin edition. See the edition published by Alfred A. Knopf, 1936, p. 159.

9. See Nina Auerbach. Bowen saw the consequences of such frustration in her family history: 'I submit that the power-loving temperament is more dangerous when it either prefers or is forced to operate in what is materially a void . . . (*BC* 455). Victoria Glendinning observes that 'The dominant figure in *The House in Paris* is . . . Mme Fisher . . . because she 'incorporates bits' of Elizabeth herself', p. 117.

10. In 'Truth and Fiction' Bowen notes how Lady Dedlock in *Bleak House* is 'tormented by the sight of the child'. Like Karen, Lady Dedlock has borne an illegitimate child whom she deserts, by a man too poor and socially inferior to be her husband, in *Afterthought*, p. 139.

11. Bowen's story, 'Tears, Idle Tears' depicts a boy of seven who cries uncontrollably at the loss of his father and the withdrawal of his mother.

12. In an unpublished piece, 'The Art of Reason or The Art of Respecting Boundries', Bowen notes that 'one can't but respect those who are straightforward truly . . . the child with its naive, disconcerting questions . . . nothing asked in innocence can offend . . . ' p. 2.

13. Bowen's story 'Kor', inspired by Rider Haggard's 'She', pictures a larger-than-life woman haunting the male imagination.

Notes to Chapter 5

1. See Sean O'Faolain, James Hall, Jocelyn Brooke, among others. Glendinning notes that this is the novel 'that many people liked best. It was a Book Society Choice. It made her some money . . . but was the one [Bowen] herself liked least' (*VG* 155–156).

2. See Heinemann, Van Duyn and Lee, who discuss the environments in which Portia lives.

3. See Hall and Lee for discussions of Anna's decoration of herself and her home.

4. Bowen has been accused of snobbery, particularly by Elizabeth Hardwick, but as Hermione Lee points out, in *The Death of the Heart* 'Bowen indicts the moneyed English middle-classes as never before',

p. 105. In a magazine piece 'The Forgotten Art of Living', Bowen clarifies what rankles her most about a lack of 'gentility': . . . 'the new rich seem, from evidence they have left, to have felt void, uncertain and gloomy – the gift [for living], therefore, was not by any means the prerogative of wealth; it was enhanced by but not always dependent upon security', p. XVIII.

5. 'The Forgotten Art of Living', p. XXVII.

6. 'The Mulberry Tree', in *Collected Impressions*, p. 193.

Notes to Chapter 6

1. See Austin and Lee, in particular.

2. Preface,'The Demon Lover', in *Collected Impressions*, p. 48. Future references will be cited in the text as *Demon*.

3. Kenney observes that 'Bowen's language of violence, destruction, and conspiracy is literal; it is no longer metaphoric' (68).

4. Autobiographical note in the Bowen collection at the Harry Ransom Humanities Research Center, University of Texas at Austin.

5. In her lecture 'The Experience of Writing', Bowen said: 'In *The Death of the Heart* and *The Heat of the Day* I have been trying to separate the true sensibility from the false. One must connect with the intelligence and the experience of the reader. I try hard to thin out the veil of language and to remember that language exists not to embroider but to define. Language must never "set" ', p. 7. She also discusses the language of the novelist at length in 'Advice' in *Afterthought*.

6. Gubar and Gilbert and Margaret Homans have explored the use of language by women writers.

7. See John Atkins for Bowen's depiction of class distinctions.

Notes to Chapter 7

1. Elizabeth Bowen, 'Out of a Book', in *Collected Impressions*, p. 269.

2. See Allen Austin, p. 19.

3. See, for example, David Daiches, Frederick R. Karl; and Hermione Lee, 12.

4. Austin, p. 20.

5. Geoffrey Wagner, p. 155.

6. 'Out of a Book', p. 265. See William Heath.

7. Elizabeth Bowen, 'Ivy Compton-Burnett' in *Collected Impressions*, p. 86.

8. See Edwin Kenney and Howard Moss.

9. Elizabeth Bowen, 'The Bend Back', *Cornhill* CLXV (Summer 1951), p. 224. Hereafter cited in the text as *BB*.

10. Elizabeth Bowen, 'Doubtful Subject', in *Collected Impressions*, p. 173.

11. Elizabeth Bowen, 'Dublin', in *Collected Impressions*, p. 181.

12. Elizabeth Bowen, 'Sources of Influence', in *Afterthought*, pp. 207–208.

13. Elizabeth Bowen, 'Uncle Silas', in *Collected Impressions*, pp. 3–4.

14. See Kenney, p. 38, for elaboration of this point.

15. Elizabeth Bowen, 'The Art of Virginia Woolf', in *Collected Impressions*, p. 81.

16. Elizabeth Bowen, 'Women's Place in the Affairs of Men', 1961. Unpublished manuscript in the Harry Ransom Humanities Research Center of the University of Texas at Austin.

17. See Kate Fullbrook.

18. See James Hall, p. 20.

19. Nancy Armstrong, p. 81.

20. Elizabeth Bowen, 'She', in *Afterthought*, p. 107.

21. Elizabeth Bowen, 'Stories by Elizabeth Bowen', in *Afterthought*, p. 77. Further references will be cited in the text as *EBS*.

22. Elizabeth Bowen, 'Stories by Katherine Mansfield', in *Afterthought*, pp. 58, 60.

23. See 'Encounters', p. 84 and 'Ann Lees', p. 91 in *Afterthought*.

24. Elizabeth Bowen, 'The Second Ghost Book', in *Afterthought*, p. 102.

25. Elizabeth Bowen, 'The Experience of Writing'.

Bibliography

Selected Works by Elizabeth Bowen

Fiction

The Hotel (London, Constable, 1927; New York, Dial, 1928; New York, Avon, 1979).
The Last September (Harmondsworth, Penguin, 1985).
Friends and Relations (Harmondsworth, Penguin, 1985).
To the North (Harmondsworth, Penguin, 1985).
The House in Paris (Harmondsworth, Penguin, 1986).
The Death of the Heart (Harmondsworth, Penguin, 1986).
The Heat of the Day (Harmondsworth, Penguin, 1986).
A World of Love (London, Cape, 1955; New York, Knopf, 1955).
The Little Girls (Harmondsworth, Penguin, 1985).
Eva Trout (Harmondsworth, Penguin, 1986).
The Collected Short Stories of Elizabeth Bowen (New York, Knopf, 1981).

Non-Fiction

Seven Winters (Dublin, Cuala Press, 1942).
Bowen's Court (London, Longmans, 1942; New York, Ecco Press, 1978).
English Novelists (London, Collins, 1942).
Collected Impressions (London, Longmans, 1950; New York, Knopf, 1949).
The Shelbourne (London, Harrap, 1951). Published as *The Shelbourne Hotel* (New York, Knopf, 1951).
A Time in Rome (London, Longmans, 1960; New York, Knopf, 1960).
Afterthought (London, Longmans, 1962; New York, Knopf, 1962).
The Good Tiger (New York, Knopf, 1965; London, Cape, 1970).

Pictures and Conversations (London, Cape, 1975; New York, Knopf, 1975).

Selected Uncollected Pieces

'The Art of Reason or The Art of Respecting Boundaries', Harry Ransom Humanities Research Center, The University of Texas at Austin.

'The Forgotten Art of Living', *Good Living*, ed. A. G. Eidenfeld (London, Contact Publications, 1948).

'Women's Place in the Affairs of Men', 1961. Unpublished ms. Harry Ransom Humanities Research Center, The University of Texas at Austin.

Selected Works about Elizabeth Bowen

Adams, Timothy Dow, 'Bend Sinister: Duration in Elizabeth Bowen's *The House in Paris*', *International Fiction Review* 7:49–52.

Atkins, John, *Six Novelists Look at Society* (London, John Calder, 1977).

Austin, Allen, *Elizabeth Bowen* (Lewisburg: Bucknell University Press, 1975).

Brantlinger, Patrick, 'Romances, Novels and Psychoanalysis', *The Practice of Psychoanalytic Criticism*, ed. Leonard Tennenhouse (Detroit, Wayne State University Press, 1978).

Daiches, David, 'Novels of Elizabeth Bowen', *English Journal* 38 (1949), 305–313.

Gill, Richard, *Happy Rural Seat: The English Country House and the Literary Imagination* (New Haven, Yale University Press, 1972).

Glendinning, Victoria, *Elizabeth Bowen: A Biography* (New York, Alfred A. Knopf, 1977).

Hall, James, *The Lunatic Giant in the Drawing Room; The British and American Novel Since 1930* (Bloomington, Indiana University Press, 1968).

Hardwick, Elizabeth, 'Elizabeth Bowen's Fiction', *Partisan Review* 16 (1949), pp.114–121.

Harkness, Bruce, 'The Fiction of Elizabeth Bowen', *English Journal*, 44 (Dec. 1955): 499–506.

Heath, William, *Elizabeth Bowen; An Introduction to Her Novels* (Madison, University of Wisconsin Press, 1961).

Heinemann, Alison, 'The Indoor Landscape in Bowen's *The Death of the Heart*', *Critique* 10 (Spring, 1968).

Karl, Frederick R, *A Reader's Guide to the Contemporary English Novel* (New York, The Noonday Press, 1962).

Kenney, Edwin J., *Elizabeth Bowen* (Lewisburg, Bucknell University Press, 1975).

Lee, Hermione, *Elizabeth Bowen: An Estimation* (London and Totowa: Vision and Barnes and Noble, 1981).

Moss, Howard, 'Review of Victoria Glendinning: *Elizabeth Bowen: A Biography*', The New Yorker, 5 February 1979, 121–128.

O'Faolain, Sean, *The Vanishing Hero: The British and American Novel Since 1930* (Bloomington, University of Indiana Press, 1968).

Van Duyn, Mona, 'Pattern and Pilgrimage: A Reading of *The Death of the Heart*', *Critique* 4 (Spring 1961): 52–66.

Wagner, Geoffrey, 'Elizabeth Bowen and the Artificial Novel', *Essays in Criticism* 13 (1963).

Selected Works of Feminist Theory and Criticism and Works about Women

Abel, Elizabeth, 'Narrative Structure(s) and Female Development: The Case of Mrs. Dalloway', *The Voyage In; Fictions of Female Development* (Hanover, University Press of New England, 1983).

Armstrong, Nancy, *Desire and Domestic Fiction: A Political History of the Novel* (New York: Oxford University Press, 1987).

Auerbach, Nina, *The Woman and the Demon: The Life of a Victorian Myth* (Cambridge: Harvard University Press, 1982).

Barrett, Michele, 'The Concept of Difference', *Feminist Review* 26 (Summer 1987), 29–41

Benjamin, Jessica, 'A Desire of One's Own: Psychoanalytic Feminism and Intersubjective Space', The University of Wisconsin-Milwaukee Center for Twentieth Century Studies Working Paper No.2 (Fall 1985).

Brownstein, Rachel M., *Becoming a Heroine: Reading About Women in Novels* (Harmondsworth, Penguin, 1984).

Chodorow, Nancy, *The Reproduction of Mothering: Psychology and the Sociology of Gender* (Berkeley: University of California Press, 1978).

Edwards, Lee R., *Psyche as Hero: Female Heroism and Fictional Form* (Middletown: Wesleyan University Press, 1984).

Farber, Ada, 'Segmentation of the Mother: Women in Greek Myth', *The Psychoanalytic Review*, 62 (1975): 29–47.

Flax, Jane, 'The Conflict Between Nurturance and Autonomy in Mother-Daughter Relationships and Within Feminism', *Feminist Studies* 4 (June 1978): 171–191.

—— 'Postmodernism and Gender Relations in Feminist Theory', *Signs*, 12 (1987): 621–643.

Foley, Helene P., ed. *Reflections of Women in Antiquity* (New York: Gordon and Breach, 1981).

Fryckstedt, Monica Correa, 'Defining the Domestic Genre: English Women Novelists of the 1850s', *Tulsa Studies in Women's Literature*, 6 (Spring 1987): 9–25.

Fullbrook, Kate, *Katherine Mansfield* (Bloomington, Indiana University Press, 1986).

Gardiner, Judith, 'On Female Identity and Writing by Women', *Writing and Sexual Difference* (Chicago, University of Chicago Press, 1982).

Gilbert, Sandra M., 'What Do Feminist Critics Want? A Postcard from the Volcano', *The New Feminist Criticism: Essays on Women, Literature, and Theory*, ed. Elaine Showalter (New York: Pantheon, 1985): 24–45.

Gilbert, Sandra M. and Gubar, Susan, *The Madwoman in the Attic. The Woman Writer and the Nineteenth Century Literary Imagination* (New Haven, Yale University Press, 1979).

—— 'Sexual Linguistics: Gender, Language, Sexuality, *New Literary History*, 16 (Spring 1985): 515–543.

Hays, H.R., *The Dangerous Sex: The Myth of Feminine Evil* (New York: Putnam's, 1964).

Hirsch, Marianne, 'Mothers and Daughters,' Signs 7: 200–222.

Homans, Margaret, *Bearing the Word: Language and Female Experience in Nineteenth-Century Women's Writing* (Chicago, University of Chicago Press, 1986).

Horney, Karen, 'The Dread of Women', *International Journal of Psychoanalysis*, 13 (1932): 348–360.

Lauter, Estelle, *Woman as Mythmaker: Poetic and Visual Art by Twentieth Century Women* (Bloomington: Indiana University Press, 1984).

Layton, Lynne, 'From Oedipus to Narcissus: Literature and the Psychology of the Self', *Mosaic* 18, 97–105.

Lefkowitz, Mary R., *Heroines and Hysterics* (London, Duckworth, 1981).

Moulton, Ruth, 'The Fear of Female Power: A Cause of Sexual Dysfunction', *Journal of the American Academy of Psychoanalysis* 5:4: 499–519.

Pomeroy, Sarah, *Goddesses, Whores, Wives, and Slaves* (New York: Schoken, 1975).

Showalter, Elaine, *A Literature of Their Own: British Women Novelists From Bronte to Lessing* (Princeton: Princeton University Press, 1977).

Stigers, Eva S., 'Sappho's Private World', *Reflections of Women in Antiquity*, ed. Helene P. Foley (New York: Gordon and Breach, 1981).

Selected Works About the Psychology and Mythology of Women

Bachofen, J.J., *Myth, Religion, and Mother Right*, trans. Ralph Manheim (Princeton: Princeton University Press, 1967).

Friedrich, Paul, *The Meaning of Aphrodite* (Chicago: University of Chicago Press, 1978).

Freud, Sigmund, 'Medusa's Head', *Collected Papers*, ed. James Strachey (New York: Basic Books, 1959).

Lederer, M.D.Wolfgang, *The Fear of Women* (New York: Harcourt, 1968).

Neumann, Erich *The Great Mother* (Princeton: Princeton University Press, 1972).

Slater, Philip *The Glory of Hera* (Boston: Beacon Press, 1968).

Index